'These days, we talk about our giant leaps forw... and development, engage in endless discussions about how AI will change our world. But one thing never changes: the women continue to get battered by the drunken husbands or the panchayat bigwigs for not following their norms. The forms and the extent seem to get bigger each day. This important study *Advanced GIS and Crime Analysis: Violence against Women in West Bengal, India* by Dr Nilanjana Chatterjee, HoD and Professor of Geography, Vidyasagar University, and her PhD scholar Priyanka Biswas will unravel many unknown facts about the crime and its extent. This book seamlessly explored the existing spatial variability of crime committed against women in West Bengal and steadily excavated the underlying determinants accountable for specific crime against women. This book competently considered both the physical and socio-economic environment to understand the situational circumstances and critically discussed emerging criminogenic issues.

This book applied GIS technologies to visualize complex crime patterns over space and suggested specific measures to curb oppression.'

— **Anirban Choudhury**, *Consulting Editor, TV 9 Bangla*

'This book comes to us at a crucial juncture in time – crime against women is on the rise and we are struggling to provide safety to women in public spaces, workplace and even their own homes. The judicious mix of qualitative, statistical, and geospatial techniques in addressing the issues as a challenging research problem brings to us, a substantial contribution to geographic literature as socio-cultural, economic, and spatial analysis have come together in this study of West Bengal, the land of the iconic Durga, symbolising feminine power. The book brings us face to face with the age-old social realities that we have not been able to wish away even in the cyber-real present-day context.'

— **Dr Sumana Bandyopadhyay**, *Professor, Department of Geography, University of Calcutta*

Advanced GIS and Crime Analysis

Advanced GIS and Crime Analysis explores the existing spatial variability of crime committed against women in West Bengal and steadily excavates the underlying determinants accountable for specific crimes against women. The book applies GIS technologies to visualise complex crime patterns over space and suggests specific measures to curb oppression.

The book applies statistical methods and GIS techniques to visualise the vulnerable areas of crime against women in West Bengal and critically discusses emerging criminogenic issues with respect to theoretical understanding and immediate situations. The determination of the most significant crime hotspots, deliberation of substantial facts through a variety of collective socio-economic as well as environmental perspectives, and suggestive measures will assist law enforcement officials, practitioners, and policymakers in adopting immediate, effective measures.

Advanced GIS and Crime Analysis will be beneficial for students of criminology, research scholars, practitioners, urban planners, and policymakers to understand the complex crime patterns that exist in West Bengal.

Priyanka Biswas holds a PhD from Vidyasagar University, West Bengal, India. Her areas of research interest are criminological studies, especially crime against women, urban environment and crime, and statistical modelling. She emphasises multidisciplinary efforts to visualise crime scenarios and evaluate policy-level change to make society crime-free.

Nilanjana Das Chatterjee is Professor and Head of the Department of Geography at Vidyasagar University, West Bengal, India. Her principal areas of research interest are environmental issues in geography, criminological analysis, and criminal psychology, with special reference to gender, urban environment, and associated socio-economic milieu. She emphasises the use of evaluation strategies to develop community-level awareness and support policy-level change to enhance the quality of society.

Advanced GIS and Crime Analysis

Violence against Women in
West Bengal, India

**Priyanka Biswas and
Nilanjana Das Chatterjee**

Routledge
Taylor & Francis Group

LONDON AND NEW YORK

First published 2024
by Routledge
4 Park Square, Milton Park, Abingdon, Oxon OX14 4RN

and by Routledge
605 Third Avenue, New York, NY 10158

Routledge is an imprint of the Taylor & Francis Group, an informa business

British Library Cataloguing-in-Publication Data
A catalogue record for this book is available from the British Library

Library of Congress Cataloging-in-Publication Data
Names: Biswas, Priyanka, author. | Das Chatterjee, Nilanjana, author.
Title: Advanced GIS and crime analysis : violence against women in West
    Bengal, India / Priyanka Biswas and Nilanjana Das Chatterjee.
Description: Abingdon, Oxon ; New York, NY : Routledge, [2025] | Includes
    bibliographical references and index.
Identifiers: LCCN 2024014946 (print) | LCCN 2024014947 (ebook) | ISBN
    9781032696034 (hardback) | ISBN 9781032696041 (paperback) | ISBN
    9781032696058 (ebook)
Subjects: LCSH: Women—Violence against—India—West Bengal. | Crime
    analysis—India—West Bengal.
Classification: LCC HV6250.4.W65 B59 2025 (print) | LCC HV6250.4.W65
    (ebook) | DDC 362.88082095414—dc23/eng/20240417
LC record available at https://lccn.loc.gov/2024014946
LC ebook record available at https://lccn.loc.gov/2024014947

ISBN: 978-1-032-69603-4 (hbk)
ISBN: 978-1-032-69604-1 (pbk)
ISBN: 978-1-032-69605-8 (ebk)

DOI: 10.4324/9781032696058

Typeset in Times new Roman
by Apex CoVantage, LLC

Contents

Figures

Tables

Foreword

Violence against women is a serious human rights violation and a public health concern. It is recognised as a 'global hidden epidemic' by the World Health Organisation. Violence against women has many forms and characteristics. Such incidents have extreme detrimental and cascading effects not only on the victim but also on the family and society. In fact, violence against women impedes and deters the working of normal life processes in our society. There are different manifestations of crime against women across different age groups and regional settings.

The present book provides an in-depth understanding of the emerging criminogenic activities that are perpetrated against women in the state of West Bengal, India. The rising incidences of gender-based atrocities against women in West Bengal have ceaselessly raised big concerns at the national and state levels among criminologists, policymakers, and social activists regarding the safeguard of women in West Bengal.

'Environmental criminology,' a branch of criminology, explains that the surrounding environment inevitably regulates people's attitudes in an area, stipulating people's criminogenic behaviour. Here the phrase 'environment' denotes the immediate physical, socio-economic, as well as psychological environment within which various crimes occur, referred by many researchers as 'context, backcloths, or situation.' Strategic space-specific location of a region and adjoining situational environment eventually affect the regional advancement or backwardness of an area and are decisive of criminogenic behaviour and regional crisis.

This book makes a scientific assertion on the rising incidences of trafficking of women and minor girls; acid attacks; sexual harassment; rape and domestic violence inflicted on women in West Bengal in the context of its case-specific hostile physiographic as well as socio-economic vulnerable environmental settings. The key purpose of this book is to portray the role of the immediate environment in perpetuating criminogenic behaviour and thereby increasing women's vulnerabilities in West Bengal. Simultaneously, the authors have also tried to suggest effective management strategies.

This book has strong methodological inputs that have been diligently applied to analyse crime against women. These include statistical methods and Geographic Information System (GIS) for the visualisation of the future potential crime areas so that possible precautionary measures may be taken in advance.

The authors have discussed critically the emerging criminogenic issues with respect to theoretical understanding and prevailing situations. The book presents an excellent exposition to the understanding of a very pertinent social evil existing in our society, that is, violence against women, and the scholars have excellently catered to the integration of theoretical and conceptual formulations necessary for spatial analysis.

I am sure that the volume will help in working out policies and strategies for fostering a society that enhances women's freedom and furthers their safety, security, and empowerment, thereby resulting in inclusive communities and societies.

October 10, 2023
Anuradha Banerjee
Professor
CSRD, SSS
Jawaharlal Nehru University
New Delhi

Acknowledgements

I am highly obliged to my co-author Professor Nilanjana Das Chatterjee, HOD, Department of Geography, Vidyasagar University, for giving valuable supervision and scholarly guidance as well as encouraging and expanding my vision and thinking during this study. I also treasured her constructive criticisms and valuable suggestions in many ways which enriched my work. Her generosity, punctuality, and unwavering support have given me a new direction in my academic life.

We greatly thank the University Grants Commission (UGC), India, and the Indian Council of Social Science Research (ICSSR, File No. Sc-2/ ICSSR/2016–17/RPS) for funding this research work.

We wish to convey our sincere gratitude to all the officials of all departments, including the National Crime Records Bureau (NCRB), Open Government Data (OGD) Platform India, Census Office, Development & Planning Department, Government of West Bengal, West Bengal Commission for Women, West Bengal State Crime Records Bureau (SCRB), Ministry of Health and Family Welfare, and other departments of state and central government for providing us valuable data and information during the intensive study.

We greatly thank the Vice Chancellor, Vidyasagar University, and the Registrar, Vidyasagar University, for their administrative support in completing this study.

We are taking this opportunity to pay respect to the teachers in the Department of Geography, Vidyasagar University, for giving their valuable suggestions, cordial support, and inspiration throughout the work. We gratefully acknowledge the help rendered in various ways by all the research scholars in our department. Their hearty assistance, cordial support, and encouragement helped us to move forward with confidence throughout the entire study. We are also thankful to the students of Geography Department, Vidyasagar University, for their great assistance during intense survey.

We are also thankful and express our sincere gratitude to all the law enforcement officials, NGOs (non-governmental organisations), self-help groups, and the local inhabitants for assisting us by providing necessary information during the field survey. We are especially thankful to all the women survivors for sharing their ghastly experiences during direct interviews with them.

We fully express our earnest gratitude to our families for their incessant support, understanding, and inspiration throughout the entire work and all the happiness, cordial affection, and love that they bring to our lives.

Abbreviations

ALRC	Asian Legal Resource Centre
ANOVA	Analysis of Variance
aOR	Adjusted Odds Ratio
ASFI	Acid Survivors Foundation of India
BDO	Block Development Officer
BJS	Bureau of Justice Statistics
BSF	Border Security Force
CCTV	Closed-circuit Television
CD Blocks	Community Development Blocks
CFA	Confirmatory Factor Analysis
CI	Confidence Interval
CIS	Commonwealth of Independent States
CrPC	Criminal Procedure Code
CRY	Child Rights and You
CSE	Commercial Sexual Exploitation
df	degree of freedom
DHDR	District Human Development Report
DOJ	Department of Justice
E	Effort
EFA	Exploratory Factor Analysis
EU	European Union
FA	Factor Analysis
FGDs	Focus Group Discussions
FIRs	First Information Reports
GDP	Gross Domestic Product
GGBK	Goranbose Gram Bikash Kendra
GIS	Geographic Information System
HDI	Human Development Index
HPI	Human Poverty Index
IPC	Indian Penal Code
IPV	Intimate Partner Violence
KMO	Kaiser–Meyer–Olkin

MOU	Memorandum of Understanding
NCPCR	National Commission for Protection of Child Rights
NCRB	National Crime Records Bureau
NDSO	National Database on Sexual Offenders
NFHS	National Family Health Survey
NGOs	Non-governmental Organisations
O	Opportunities
P	Pay off
PC	Principal Component
PCA	Principal Component Analysis
PCP	Parallel Coordinate Plot
PCR	Principal Component Regression
POCSO	Protection of Children from Sexual Offence
PPP	Public–Private–Partnership
PS	Police Station
PWDVA	Protection of Women from Domestic Violence Act
QQ Plot	quantile–quantile plot
R	Risk
RPF	Railway Protection Force
RRR	Relative Risk Ratio
SALSA	State Legal Services Authority
SCRB	State Crime Record Bureau
SD	Standard Deviation
SEM	Social–Ecological Model
SHGs	Self-Help Groups
SLL	Special & Local Law
UNICEF	United Nations International Children's Emergency Fund
UNODC	United Nations Office on Drug and Crime
USDOS	United States Department of State
VIF	Variance Inflation Factor
WHO	World Health Organisation

1 Introduction

Definition and Conceptual Framework of Crime against Women

Today's world is gravitating with one of the most decisive forms of bestiality against human beings, that is, 'Crime against Women.' The phrase 'Crime against Women' refers to those crimes that are directed specifically against women and involve physical, sexual, and emotional maltreatment and assault of women. It is one of the most systematic and widespread human rights issues in the present world and is prevalent in all human societies, irrespective of race, religion, socio-economic status, and culture. This widespread human rights violation sometimes transcends national, cultural, racial, and class boundaries; affects every society; and is a major obstacle to ending gender inequality and discrimination globally (UN General Assembly, 1993). The UN Declaration on the Elimination of Violence against Women (1993) defines crime against women as

> any act of gender-based violence that results in, or is likely to be result in, physical, sexual or psychological harm or suffering to women, including threats of such acts, coercion or arbitrary deprivation of liberty, whether occurring in public or in private life.

It may scar the early years of life of a woman in the form of child abuse, incest, and sexual harassment; it may threaten marriage and family as well as social life, sometimes culminating in murder or suicide. The most decisive forms of violence that the women faced during their whole lifespan are graphically represented in Figure 1.1. Most often, spouses, other intimate partners, husband's relatives, parents, own kin's and relatives, neighbours, even the unknown roadside Romeos, owner or employer, and office colleagues become the potential perpetrators to hurt women physically as well as psychologically and bring misfortune to women's lives. The effects of violence can be subversive to a woman's reproductive health as well as to other aspects of her physical and mental well-being. Besides causing physical injuries, brutality

DOI: 10.4324/9781032696058-1

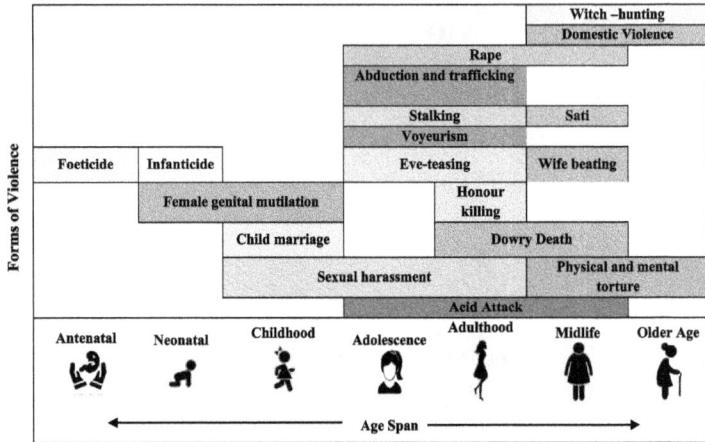

Figure 1.1 Most Significant Forms of Crime against Women

may increase long-term health-related difficulties among women, including physical disabilities, chronic pains, psychological disorders, drug and alcohol abuses, chronic depressions, unintended pregnancies, miscarriages, sexually transmitted diseases, and other kinds of adverse outcomes, and thereby adversely affect the progress of the society.

Relevance of the Study

Crime against women is manifested as a worldwide epidemic. It is a century-old phenomenon that has been perpetrated in the name of religion, social customs, and rituals. Internationally, one in every three women has been beaten, coerced into sex, or abused in their lifetime by a member of their own family (Heise et al., 1999). Worldwide, the most pervasive form of violence perpetrated against women is domestic violence (Heise et al., 1994). According to the Bureau of Justice Statistics (BJS) report, domestic violence manifested victimisations committed by current or former intimate partners, immediate family members (parents, children, or siblings), and other relatives (Truman & Morgan, 2014). Another most common form of violence against women is intimate partner violence performed by husbands or intimate male partners or ex-partners. Intimate partner violence refers to any behaviour within an intimate relationship that causes physical, psychological, emotional, or sexual harm and various controlling behaviours to those in the relationship. Payne and Wermeling (2009) in their study highlighted the US Department of Justice's (DOJ) 2008 report, which reflects that domestic and intimate partner violence occurs in an epidemic proportion throughout the world, affecting nearly 6.2 million American women each year and causing serious injury which is more severe than car accidents, muggings, and rape combined. As per the global estimates published by the World Health Organisation (WHO), the prevalence of intimate partner violence ranges from 23.2% in high-income nations, to 24.6% in the WHO Western Pacific region, to 37% in the WHO Eastern Mediterranean region, and to 37.7% in the WHO South-East Asia region (WHO, 2013). Besides, internationally, 7% of women have been facing sexual assault by someone other than a partner (WHO, 2013). Yet the availability of data for non-partner sexual assault is very limited. As per the European Union (EU)-wide survey report (European Union Agency for Fundamental Rights, 2014), one in every ten women has experienced some form of physical and/or sexual assault since the age of 15. According to UNICEF (United Nations International Children's Emergency Fund) (2017), worldwide around 15 million adolescent girls aged 15–19 have experienced forced sex at some point of their life. Most of the time, adolescent girls are at risk of forced sex by the current or former spouse, partner, or boyfriend. And it is so astonishing that only 1% of ever-tortured women or girls seek professional help (UNICEF, 2017). The practice of child marriage is also a worldwide issue of concern in the present days. The global report of UNICEF in 2018 on child marriage highlights that during the past decade, the practice of underage marriage has been following a declining trend. Still, worldwide, approximately 650 million women and girls today were married before age 18 (UNICEF, 2018). Especially in West and Central Africa, this harmful practice of child marriage is almost a very common issue, where four in every ten women were married before 18 years of age (UNICEF, 2018). Moreover, women throughout the world have been facing another decisive form of violence, that is, human trafficking. As per a senior coordinator for International Women's Issues (1998), each year more than 1 million women and children are trafficked globally for the purpose of domestic servitude, forced labour, and commercial sexual exploitation (CSE). As per the United Nations Office on Drugs and Crime report (UNODC, 2012), sexual exploitation is closely associated with women trafficking. From 2007 to 2010, among all the detected victims of trafficking, sexual abuse accounted for approximately 57–60% (UNODC, 2012). Trafficking of women has become a universal organised crime which is not limited to underdeveloped or developing countries like India, Nepal, Bangladesh, and other Commonwealth of Independent States (CIS) but rather extend its wings towards the developed world. Another most decisive form of gender-based atrocity that women are facing in recent days is acid attacks. It is considered a form of 'intimate terrorism' as it involves deliberately throwing chemical solution onto another person with an intention of disfiguring that person out of jealousy and/or revenge (Welsh, 2009). It is mostly predominant in the developing world, especially in South Asian countries like Bangladesh, India, Pakistan, and Cambodia (Das et al., 2013; Sharma, 2005). Yet, the study conducted by the Avon Global Centre for Women and Justice (2011) reveals that in recent days, acid attacks have become a major human rights viola-tion issue throughout the world, including the United States and Great Britain. Hence, in these present circumstances, women organisations throughout the world have drawn their core attention to address oppression against women. And through their continuous efforts, crime against women has now become an international issue of concern.

Scenarios in India

In the context of India, crime against women is one of the major societal issues of concern. It is a century-old phenomenon in Indian society that is spatially distributed in every state and is deep-rooted in every hierarchical level of soci-ety. The issue of violation against women rears its nasty head from time to time in the form of abduction, rape, gang rape, cruelty by husbands and relatives, acid attacks, honour killings, and so on (Oberoi, 2017). According to a histori-cal observation, in Indian culture, women were worshipped as 'DEVI' or God-dess. Yet, Indian women find themselves completely oppressed and subjugated in a patriarchal society. Here women do not enjoy all the freedom stated in the Indian Constitution. In Indian patriarchal society, women are treated as infe-rior to men (Narasimhan, 1994; Johnson & Johnson, 2001). In the patriarchal society, men often mark the mental boundaries of power between women and themselves based on the appearance and sexuality of women (Anwary, 2003). Hence, men never accept the conceit and superiority of women and try to exert their masculine power over women to keep them in their place (Anwary, 2003). As per the National Family Health Survey (NFHS-3) report, about 35% of women in India have experienced some or the other form of physical or sexual violence within the age group of 15–49 years (International Institute for Popu-lation Sciences (IIPS) and Macro International, 2007). The NFHS-3 report also reveals that about 37% of ever-married women have experienced some form of physical or sexual violence by their husband. Yet, the NFHS-4 report (Interna-tional Institute for Population Sciences (IIPS) and ICF, 2017) shows a declining trend of spousal physical or sexual violence (31%) compared to the NFHS-3 report (37%). Nonetheless, no changes have been found in women's experience of spousal abuse during the 12 months preceding each survey (i.e., 24% in both the NFHS-3 and NFHS-4 report). As per the National Crime Records Bureau (NCRB, 2014), a crime against women is recorded every 1.7 minutes in India. Every 16 minutes a rape case is recorded, and every 4.4 minutes a woman is sub-jected to domestic violence. In recent days, even infants and children have been subjected to rape, sexual exploitation, and other forms of violations (Oberoi, 2017). As per the NCRB, in 2016, a total of 3,38,954 cases (both IPC and SLL) of crime against women were reported in India as compared to 3,27,394 cases in 2015, which shows an increase of 3.5% over the year 2015 (NCRB, 2016).

If the NCRB reports of the last seven years are considered, it can be observed that crime against women in India has increased continuously from 2010 to 2014, with 2,13,585 cases registered in 2010 and 3,37,922 in 2014. Though in 2015 the number of registered cases declined slightly (decreased by 3.1% over 2014), it again increased in 2016 with 3,38,954 cases. The rate of crime against women also increased during this period.

As per the 2016 NCRB report, the top three states regarding crime against women are Uttar Pradesh (49,262 cases; share 14.5% of all India records), followed by West Bengal (32,513 cases; share 9.6% of all India records), and Maharashtra (31,388 cases; share 9.3% of all India records). Delhi UT (Union Territory) reported the highest crime rate (160.4) in 2016 compared to the all-India average (rate of 55.2). Among the 19 metropolitan cities in India, Delhi holds the leading position (rate of 182.1, share of 33.1% of the national total), followed by Lucknow (159.8), Jaipur (144.1), and Patna (133.8). State-wise, distinct spatial patterns of crime against women in India can also be observed. For instance, as per the 2016 NCRB report, Madhya Pradesh reported the highest occurrence of 'rape' (Sec. 376, 376C, and 376D IPC) cases (4,882), followed by Uttar Pradesh (4,816) and Maharashtra (4,189), whereas West Bengal has been accounted for the maximum reported incidences of 'cruelty by husband or his relatives' (Sec. 498A IPC) (19,302), followed by Rajasthan (13,811) and Uttar Pradesh (11,159). For the incidence of 'Dowry deaths' (Sec. 304B IPC), Uttar Pradesh has reported the highest number of cases (2,473), followed by Bihar (987), Madhya Pradesh (629), and West Bengal (535). Maharashtra has been in the foremost position regarding cases registered under the crime head of 'assault on women with intent to outrage her modesty' (Sec. 354, 354-A, 354-B, 354-C, 354-D IPC). Uttar Pradesh and Madhya Pradesh followed closely, with 11,335 and 8,717 reported cases, respectively. The highest number of 'kidnapping and abduction of women' (Sec. 363, 363-A, 364, 364-A, 365, 366, 366-A, 366-B, 367, 368, and 369 IPC) cases have been reported from Uttar Pradesh (12,994), Maharashtra (6,170), and Bihar (5,496). In 2016, a total of 8,132 cases of 'Human trafficking' (Sec. 370 and 370-A IPC) were reported across India, whereas West Bengal ranked 1st with 3,579 reported cases, accounting for 44% of the national share. It is noteworthy that as per the NCRB 2016 report, a sharp change has been observed in the incidence of rape compared to a rise in other crime heads of violations against women. While overall crime against women in India has risen just by only 3%, incidents of rape have gone up by 12.4%, from 34,651 cases in 2015 to 38,947 in 2016. Despite this, it is so astonishing that in India wife beating is considered justifiable. As per the last exhaustive family survey (NFHS-4; 2015–2016) conducted by the Ministry of Health and Family Welfare in India, more than 54% of men and 51% of women agreed that it was acceptable for a man to beat his wife if she disrespects her in-laws, neglects her home or children, goes out of home without informing her husband, is suspected of being unfaithful, refuses to have sex, and so on. Even in most cases, crimes against women go unreported for understandable reasons like attached social stigmas, distrust in legal mechanisms, fear of retaliation, and so on. More often, women themselves agree with the fact that their own subjection to violence is largely shaped by their own violence-supportive attitudes (Flood & Pease, 2009). Various new legislations have been brought, and amendments have been made to the existing IPC (Indian Penal Code) and CrPC (Criminal Procedure Code) after the brutal 2012 'Delhi Nirbhaya gang rape and murder case' (Natarajan, 2016; Biswas & Chatterjee, 2017); civil law protections are also available in India with a view to handle these crimes efficiently. These are broadly classified into two categories: (1) the crimes under the Indian Penal Code and (2) the crimes under the Special and Local Laws (SLL). The Protection of Women from Domestic Violence Act (PWDVA), 2005, has been introduced in this respect. The Indian parliament promulgated the Criminal Law (Amendment) Act, 2013, which incorporated acid attacks, sexual harassment, voyeurism, and stalking into the IPC. The Indian parliament has also promulgated the Sexual Harassment of Women at Workplace (Prevention, Prohibition and Redressal) Act, 2013, which provides protection to working women at the workplace and is popularly recognised as 'Visakha Guidelines.' The Government of India has been making rigorous efforts to address the gender gap and lessen violence against women in India. The weakened laws and regulations, ineffectiveness of the legal justice system, gender discrimination, and, above all, the male-dominated patriarchal society in India act as catalysts to put women at high risk of victimisation.

Women Susceptibilities in West Bengal

Gender-related atrocities in West Bengal are deeply rooted in patriarchal culture. From the 'Sati' period to the modern era, gender-related atrocities still prevail in many areas of this state in the form of sex-selective abortion, infanticide, child abuse, early age of marriage, domestic abuse, dowry death, cruelty by husband and his relatives, sexual atrocities, forced prostitution, kidnapping, women trafficking, honour killing, rape, acid attacks, and many other forms of brutality. As per the 2016 NCRB report, West Bengal ranks second in terms of brutalities committed against women in India, with 32,513 reported cases (IPC + SLL) after Uttar Pradesh (49,262 cases) (NCRB, 2016). It can be observed from the last seven years of NCRB data that since 2010, the rate of crime committed against women in West Bengal has been on a rising trend, from, 29% in 2010 to 71.2% in 2016.

A complete spatial variability has been observed in West Bengal regarding the oppression that women face in their daily life. According to the 2015 district-wise open government data provided by the Ministry of Home Affairs (data.gov.in), in West Bengal crime against women is mostly predominant in the districts of North-24 and South-24 Parganas, Nadia, Murshidabad, Howrah, Bardhaman, and Kolkata (map shown in Figure 1.2). If the district-wise data (data.gov.in) of the last 14 years (2002–2015) are considered, it can be observed that the occurrence of crime against women is higher in the above-mentioned districts (Figure 1.3). Among the metropolitan cities in India, Kolkata, the capital of West Bengal, lies in a vulnerable position (24.9 rate) regarding violence committed against women (NCRB, 2016).

The most widespread form of violence that the women in West Bengal have experienced in their daily life is the cruelties by husband or his relatives (Sec. 498A IPC). As per the NCRB report, in 2016, West Bengal ranks highest with 19,302 recorded incidences of cruelties perpetrated by women's husbands or his relatives (NCRB, 2016). According to the 2014 district-wise open government data (data.gov.in), in West Bengal the district North-24 Parganas (3,569 cases) lies in the top position regarding cruelties by husband or his relatives, followed by South-24 Parganas, Murshidabad, Nadia, Howrah, Hooghly, Bardhaman, and Kolkata. Another most leading crime that put women's lives from heaven to grave in Bengal is human trafficking. Trafficking of poor, innocent, and naive minor girls and women, specifically from the remote rural parts of West Bengal, for commercial gain, has been following an ever-rising trend since the recent past. According to the NCRB report, in 2016, West Bengal reported the highest numbers of human trafficking cases (3,579 out of the total 8,132 cases reported in India), which accounts for 44.01% of the national total (NCRB, 2016). The NCRB data reveals that for the reported cases of human trafficking (370 and 370A IPC), Kolkata in West Bengal occupied the top position (particularly the women cases) during 2016 (NCRB, 2016). Moreover, the districts of Howrah, Murshidabad, North-24 and South-24 Parganas, Purba Medinipur, Birbhum, North and South Dinajpur, Jalpaiguri, and Darjeeling have been identified as the major hotbed of trafficking. The geographically distinct location of this state makes it a convenient transit point for child and women trafficking to other states of India and to foreign destinations for camel jockeying, organ trading, begging, forced prostitution, and many other filthy jobs. Apart from trafficking, West Bengal has been experiencing an alarming rate of incidences of kidnapping and abduction of minor girls and women (Sec. 363–369 IPC and 371–373 IPC). According to the NCRB report, in 2016, a total of 8,672 cases of kidnapping and abduction (female cases only) were reported in West Bengal, which reflects an increase of about 2.28% as compared to the previous year's report (5,889 cases) (NCRB, 2016). It is astonishingly observed that in 2016, out of 3,14,674 missing women in India, 53,654 were from West Bengal only (NCRB, 2016). Even so, about 39,124 women remain totally untraced (NCRB, 2016). Social activists conveyed that a close association exists between missing persons and organised crime trafficking. Another noticeable offence that is happening covertly in many areas

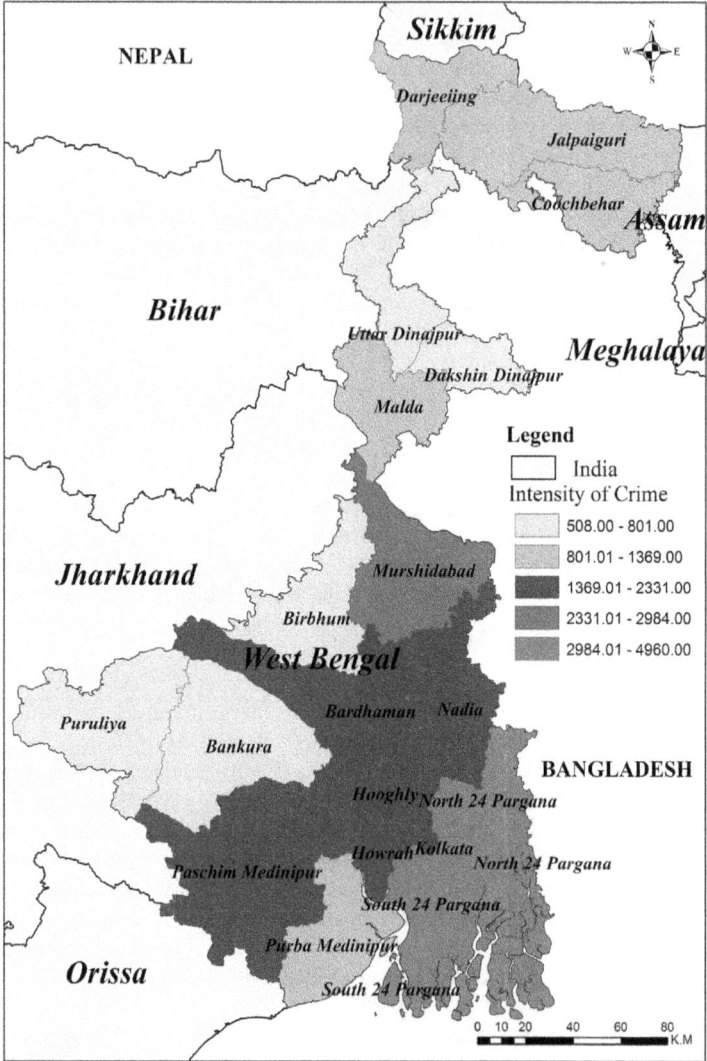

Figure 1.2 District-wise Spatial Expansion of Crime against Women in West Bengal in 2015

Source: data.gov.in, 2015

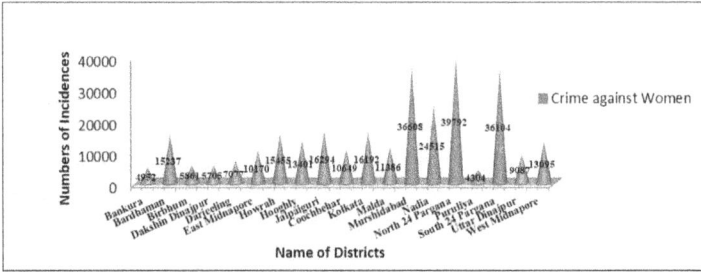

Figure 1.3 District-wise Reported Incidences of Crime against Women in West Bengal from 2002 to 2015

Source: data.gov.in

of West Bengal is child marriage. As per the NFHS-4 (2015–2016) report, West Bengal occupies the top position concerning the prevalence of under-age marriage among 15–19-year-old girls and 20–24-year-old women, with 25.6% and 41.6%, respectively. The National Commission for Protection of Child Rights (NCPCR, 2018) released a report 'National analysis of child marriage and teenage pregnancy' based on NFHS-4 data (2015–2016), which reveals that among the top 100 high-prevalence districts of child marriage in India, the Murshidabad district in West Bengal shows the highest occurrence (39.9%) of underage marriage. This report identified 14 districts in West Bengal, including Murshidabad (39.9%), Birbhum (35.2%), North-24 Parganas (31.4%), and Nadia (30.8%), where the practice of child marriage is highly prevalent (NCPCR, 2018). Activists conveyed that underage marriage is one of the most effective means of trafficking used by the traffickers as it remains secretive and often hard to measure. Apart from the above-mentioned crimes, in 2016, a total of 1,110 rape (376, 376C, 376D IPC) cases and 1,646 attempts to commit rape (376/511 IPC) cases were reported in West Bengal (NCRB, 2016). According to the district-wise open government data (data.gov.in), in 2014, the districts of Murshidabad (474 cases) reported the highest number of rape cases, followed by South-24 Parganas (341), North-24 Parganas (328), Malda (252), Jalpaiguri (247), and North Dinajpur (187). And for the attempt to commit rape cases (376/511 IPC), the districts of Murshidabad (325), Nadia (230), South-24 Parganas (138), North-24 Parganas (135), Bardhaman (134), North Dinajpur (130), and Malda (119) were identified as the major hotbed in regard to incidence reported. Recently, another notorious form of crime that has expanded its wings and brought misfortune among the young women and girls in West Bengal is 'Acid attacks.' As per the NCRB report, in 2016, West Bengal ranks first in India for acid attacks on women, with 76 reported cases (NCRB, 2016). The district-wise open government data, 2014 (data.gov.in), reveals that such a form of gender-based atrocity is predominant in South

Bengal, specifically in the districts of East Medinipur, Paschim Medinipur, North-24 Parganas, South-24 Parganas, Bardhaman, Hugli, North Dinajpur, and Dakshin Dinajpur. Many young lives are completely ruined and die a hundred deaths physically and psychologically owing to such kinds of intimate terrorism. Thus, in the present-day context, it is apparent that the safety of women in West Bengal has become a matter of concern. Another notable thing is that not all the districts in West Bengal are equally vulnerable regarding the intensity of crime against women. The most crime-prone districts are Murshidabad, North-24 and South-24 Parganas, Malda, Nadia, Bardhaman, North Dinajpur, Kolkata, Howrah, Jalpaiguri, and North and South Dinajpur. Besides, a complete spatial variability is observed in West Bengal in terms of crime specificity. Specific forms of crimes against women are concentrated in specific pockets in West Bengal. For instance, trafficking in women and minors is found to be very active in the border areas of West Bengal. Overall, in the present-day context, the safety of women in West Bengal has become a matter of grave concern.

Aim of This Book

This book aims to take a glimpse into the existing scenario of crime against women in West Bengal, understand women's susceptibility issues from socio-economic, geographic, and environmental perspectives, identify and characterise crime 'hotspots' using Geographical Information Systems (GIS) technologies, predict potentially vulnerable areas of crime using geovisual analytical tools for policy implementation, and suggest some situational crime prevention measures to lessen crime against women in West Bengal.

Deliberation of the Study Area

Study area selection is a vital part of any research work. In social science, the researchers focus on specific social problem(s) in an area. Research questions and study objectives are set looking at the problem(s) which the researchers think to mitigate and execute strategies for. Research problems arise for many reasons. Exact space-specific factors or say the situational environment is sometimes accountable for upheaving adverse situations and giving birth to socio-economic adversities of that area. Hostile physiographic location, constant exposure to natural calamities, unfavourable infrastructural set-up, and poor socio-economic conditions sometimes result in impoverishing social structure, breaking the social ties, lamenting socio-economic imbalances, and nourishing anti-social behaviour in a society that make the region vulnerable. Therefore, criminogenic activities might have emerged in a region. The physical vulnerabilities in a region have an enormous role in enhancing the socio-economic vulnerabilities of that region, eventually affecting the impoverished groups in society and making them involved in anti-social behaviour. The impact of adverse physiographic settings has always been vindictive to the local communities. It may be due to the borderland location that extreme exposure to natural calamities is evident in socio-economic susceptibilities that alter the social behavioural pattern and expose the local inhabitants to involve in risky criminogenic activities. Thus, to understand the smack of swelling attitudes towards antisocial behaviour in a region and the execution of effective management strategies, a scientific assertion on the concerned physiographic as well as associated socio-economic circumstances is required. In this backcloth, this study intends to provide a cogent understanding of the emerging criminogenic activities perpetrated against women in West Bengal, considering its specific hostile physiographic as well as socio-economically vulnerable settings. A brief discussion about the study area (Figure 1.4) is given below.

Physiographic Settings of West Bengal

West Bengal is well-known for its diversified physiographical settings. The *Darjeeling Himalayan Hill Region* in the northern extremity of the state is part of the Eastern Himalayan Mountain range. The 'Sandakfu' (height: 3,636 m) is the highest pick in this region. The entire Darjeeling district (except Siliguri subdivision) and a narrow northern portion of Jalpaiguri district form this hilly region. This hilly region starts abruptly from the Tarai *region*, which separates the hills from the North Bengal plains. The North Bengal plains are silt-laden plains, starting from the south of the *Tarai region*, stretching up to the left bank of the Ganges River, and gradually transitioning into the Ganges Delta towards the south. The Rarh region lies between the western plateau and highlands in the west and the Ganges delta in the east. The coastal region in the southern extreme, with the Sundarbans mangrove forest, forms the geographical landmark at the Ganges Delta and makes the state of West Bengal extremely diversified in nature.

Methodology

Data Sources

To conduct the entire study, both primary and secondary data sources have been considered to accumulate the necessary information. Fact-finding direct field interviews with the respondents, focus group discussions (FGDs) with the activists, and case studies have been considered primary data sources. On the contrary, the NCRB reports, the National Family Health Survey (NFHS-4) reports, the district-level open government data (data.gov.in), First Information

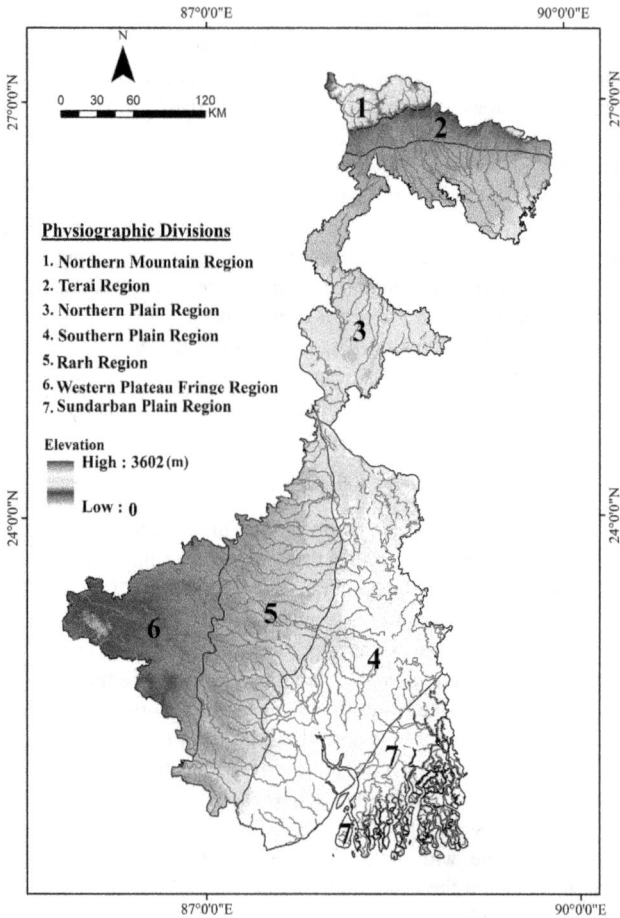

Figure 1.4 Study Area

Reports (FIR), Women Commission reports, District Human Development Report (DHDR), NGO records, census reports, and so on have been considered secondary data sources. The data sources for the required information is summarised in Table 1.1.

Variables of Interest

The variables included in this study have been categorised into two parts: dependent variables and independent variables. Dependent variables delineate

Table 1.1 Data Sources

Data Types	Data Used	Data Sources
Secondary data	The National Family Health Survey 2015–2016 (NFHS-4) report on crimes committed against women	Ministry of Health and Family Welfare
	Crime statistics in India	NCRB (National Crime Record Bureau)
	Crime data in West Bengal	West Bengal State Crime Record Bureau (SCRB)
	Recorded reports in Women Commission	West Bengal Commission for Women
	Women literacy data	Census report
	District HDI data	Development and Planning Department, Government of West Bengal
	Newspaper records	Well-circulated newspapers: *The Times of India*, *The Telegraph*, *Ananda Bazar Patrika*, *The Hindustan Times*, etc.
Primary data	Empirical datasets	Community-based cross-sectional surveys, FGDs, and case studies

the crime rates, and independent variables are those that act as catalysts to create situational environment and intensify vulnerability among women. The independent variables for this study have been collected under four major aspects based on a theoretical understanding of criminogenic activities. These aspects include (a) understanding criminogenic concern considering the social disorganisation concept (Shaw & McKay, 1942), (b) considering crime events in regard to the opportunity of crime (Rational Choice theory, Cornish & Clarke, 1986), (c) measuring the routine activities of both the offender(s) and victim(s) (Routine Activity theory, Cohen & Felson, 1979), and (d) considering the physiographic environmental settings (Environmental Criminological approach, Brantingham & Brantingham, 1980) for ample understanding of spatial variability of crime against women in West Bengal. Under the first aspect, the variables include economic deprivation or poverty, employment status, social isolation, neighbourhood control, residential mobility, racial or ethnic heterogeneity, educational status, and family disruption. Under the crime opportunity aspect, the considered variables are the regulatory capacity of administration, surveillance systems (presence or absence of CCTV cameras, street lights), political support, social systems, the physical design of the landscape, and so on. The variables considered under the third aspect, that is, measuring routine activities, are alcohol or drug abuse, lifestyle, awareness space, peer groups, and so on. Under the physiographic environmental aspect, the considered variables incorporate geographical disadvantageous location, poor accessibility and connectivity, resource unavailability, sharing of porous national and international borders, and increasing women's vulnerabilities. These independent variables have been derived from the fact-finding interviews, FGDs, field observations, and other secondary data sources. Moreover, GIS tools have been used to generate crime maps, and different statistical techniques have been used to analyse the crime patterns more conveniently. These forward-thinking and proactive methods, technologies, and GIS tools enable investigators to focus on their resources, take immediate, effective measures, and prevent crime and social harm. A general methodological overview of the entire study has been provided through a flowchart reflected in Figure 1.5. The methodologies followed in each chapter for specific crime types have been discussed in detail later.

Significant Contribution of This Study

Crime against women is one of the most pervasive forms of human rights violations worldwide. Every society has faced these challenges in recent days. Women belonging to every societal and economic class, ethnicity, culture, and even geographic region are more or less victims of such a crucial issue. Experience of violence or the threat of violence and assaults in public and private space terrorises many women; destroys their dignity, self-respect, security, and freedom; and keeps them from freely involving in social activities. In many cases, our society is responsible for generating gender-based violence by implementing social norms. The typical patriarchal social system practised such male supremacy over females in every aspect. These situations in our society actually opened up a new dimension of further research. This study involves the determination of major crime hotspots for each crime type perpetrated against women in West Bengal and situational environmental consideration of crime, that is, how the surrounding socio-physical environment provides the opportunities for offenders to commit crime in a specific area. This study will make people more concerned about gender-biased practices in our society. It will make people aware of their own societal views about women. Do women in our society feel safe? Which types of violence do women face in society most? What are the social–environmental factors motivating the offenders to commit crimes against women in society? This awareness among the people in our society may trim down the practice in a broad sense. Even in our society, women are too much unaware about their legal rights. Even the Indian patriarchal social system and culture make women believe that they themselves are responsible for their fate. The attached social stigma and fear of being a victim again restrict women from reporting to the police. This study may acknowledge that gender-based atrocities and assaults are not only a crime and not an affront to a woman's chastity; they are also a violation of women's human rights and their dignity.

Data from Published Sources	Unpublished	Case Study	Interview

Published NCRB data

Published WB SCRB

FIR Reports

Newspaper Reports

Census Reports

Published DHDR data

Published NFHS data

Literature Review

Status of women past and present scenario

Identification of research problem

Identification of vulnerable region in WB

Community-based cross-sectional observational study

Generate primary database

Data from secondary sources

Use Statistical tools

Understanding spatial pattern of crime

Consider the significance of the socio-economic and environmental aspects of crime

Identify the Vulnerable Area

Hotspot analysis and crime mapping

Significance of risk factor measure by

1. PCA (Principal Component Analysis)
2. Multivariate Logistic Regression

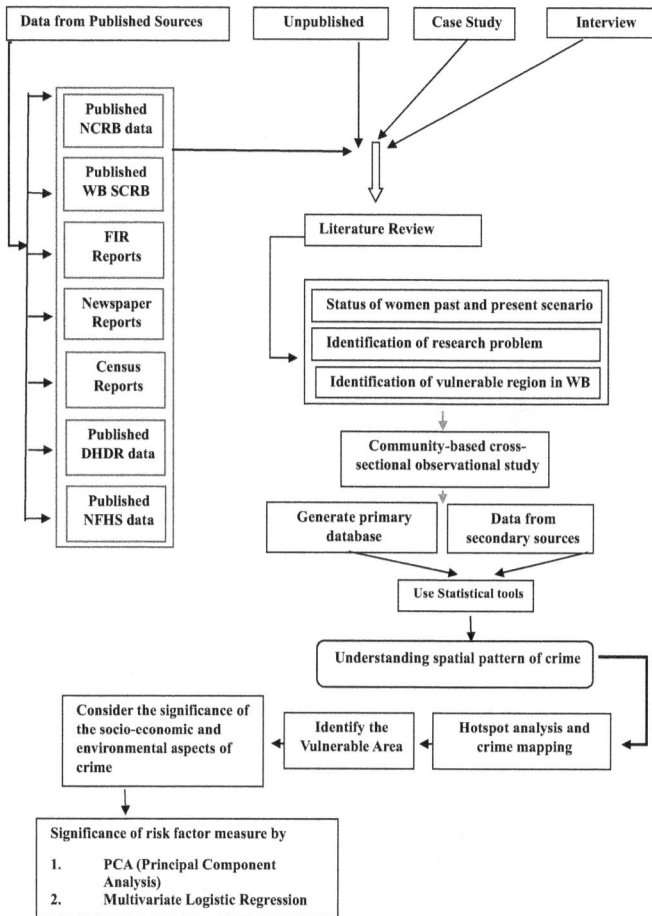

Figure 1.5 Overall Methodological Flowchart

This study will make women aware of their surrounding places where the situational environmental conditions may provide opportunities for the offender(s) to commit crime, so that they can avoid those places. Besides, this study would encourage women to report incidents to the police and take legal action against the offenders. This study would help law enforcement officials to better understand which specific areas are more susceptible to criminogenic nuisance and the factors responsible for such activities so that they could take the necessary measures to minimise the rate of crime in those particular areas. Such analysis of crime may contribute to a better under-standing of crime patterns to support better policing through better target-ing patrols and improved investigations. Thus, by limiting opportunities (O) (e.g., employing more security guards and increasing police patrolling, using security surveillance, namely CCTV cameras, good streetlights, improved neighbourhood watch, increasing awareness among people), increasing risk (R) (e.g., risk of being caught), increasing effort (E), and reducing the payoff (P), crime will decrease.

References

Anwary, A. (2003). Acid violence and medical care in Bangladesh: Women's activism as carework. *Gender & Society, 17*(2), 305–313.

Avon Global Centre for Women and Justice at Cornell Law School. (2011). *Combating acid violence in Bangladesh, India, and Cambodia.* New York City Bar, Cornell University Law School, Virtue Foundation.

Biswas, P., & Chatterjee, N. D. (2017). Spatial distributional pattern of eve-teasing in urban area; Mapping for security, safety and prevention – A case study of Asansol Municipal Area, West Bengal, India. *Indian Cartogra-pher, 37,*127–135.

Brantingham, P. J., & Brantingham, P. L. (1980). Crime, occupation, and economic specialization. In D. E. Georges-Abeyie & K. D. Harries (Eds.), *Crime: A spatial perspective* (pp. 93–108). Columbia University Press. https://doi.org/10.7312/geor90788-011.

Cohen, L. E., & Felson, M. (1979). Social change and crime rate trends: A routine activity approach. *American Sociological Review, 44,* 588–608.

Cornish, D., & Clarke, R. (1986). Situational prevention, displacement of crime and rational choice theory. In Heal K., Laycock G. K. (Eds.). *Situ-ational crime prevention: From theory into practice* (pp. 1–16). Richmond, UK: Her Majesty's Stationery Office.

Das, K. K., Khondokar, M. S., Quamruzzaman, M., Ahmed, S. S., & Peck, M. (2013). Assault by burning in Dhaka, Bangladesh. *Burns, 39*(1), 177–183.

European Union Agency for Fundamental Rights. (2014). *Violence against women: An EU-wide survey.* Retrieved February 12, 2019, from www.ref-world.org/docid/5316ef6a4.html

Flood, M., & Pease, B. (2009). Factors influencing attitudes to violence against women. *Trauma, Violence, & Abuse, 10*(2), 125–142.

Heise, L., Ellsberg, M., & Gottemoeller, M. (1999). Ending violence against women. *Population Reports, 27*(4).

Heise, L., Pitanguy, J., & Germain, A. (1994). *Violence against women: The hidden health burden* (World Bank discussion papers 255). The World Bank.

International Institute for Population Sciences and ICF. (2017). National Fam-ily Health Survey (NFHS-4), 2015–16: India. Mumbai: IIPS.

International Institute for Population Sciences (IIPS) and Macro International. (2007). National Family Health Survey (NFHS-3), 2005–06: India. Mumbai: IIPS.

Johnson, P. S., & Johnson, J. A. (2001). The oppression of women in India. *Violence against Women*, *7*(9), 1051–1068.

Narasimhan, S. (1994). India: From sati to sex-determination tests. In M. Davies (Ed.), *Women and violence* (pp. 43–52). Zed Books.

Natarajan, M. (2016). Rapid assessment of "eve teasing" (sexual harassment) of young women during the commute to college In India. *Crime Science*, *5*(1), 6. https://doi.org/10.1186/s40163-016-0054-9.

National Commission for Protection of Child Rights (NCPCR). (2018, September 4). *National analysis of child marriage and teenage pregnancy based on NFHS-4 (2015–16)*. Government of India.

NCRB. (2014). *Crime in India: Statistics-2014*. National Crime Records Bureau, Ministry of Home Affairs, Government of India. https://ncrb.gov.in/en

NCRB. (2016). *Crime in India: Statistics-2016*. National Crime Records Bureau, Ministry of Home Affairs, Government of India. https://ncrb.gov.in/en

Oberoi, R. (2017, May 28). Fighting for survival as a woman. *The Citizen*. Retrieved June 12, 2018, from www.thecitizen.in/index.php/en/NewsDetail/index/10/10782/Fighting-for-Survival-as-a-Woman

Open Government Data, Government of India. https://data.gov.in/

Payne, D., & Wermeling, L. (2009). Domestic violence and the female victim: The real reason women stay. *Journal of Multicultural, Gender and Minority Studies*, *3*(1), 1–6.

Senior Coordinator for International Women's Issues. (1998). Trafficking in women and girls – An international human rights violation: Fact Sheet, US Department of State, Washington, DC. *Trends in Organized Crime*, *3*(4), 21–23.

Sharma, B. R. (2005). Social etiology of violence against women in India. *The Social Science Journal*, *42*(3), 375–389.

Shaw, C. R., & McKay, H. D. (1942). *Juvenile delinquency and urban areas*. University of Chicago Press.

Truman, J. L., & Morgan, R. E. (2014). *Nonfatal domestic violence* (Special Report). BJS, U.S. Department of Justice. https://bjs.ojp.gov/content/pub/pdf/ndv0312.pdf

UN General Assembly. (1993). *Declaration on the elimination of violence against women*. United Nations.

UNICEF. (2017). *A familiar face: Violence in the lives of children and adolescents*. UNICEF. Retrieved January 12, 2018, from https://data.unicef.org/resources/a-familiar-face/

UNICEF. (2018). *Child marriage: Latest trends and future prospects*. UNICEF. Retrieved July 12, 2019, from https://data.unicef.org/resources/child-marriage-latest-trends-and-future-prospects/

United Nations Office on Drugs and Crime (UNODC). (2012). *What is human trafficking?* Retrieved June 15, 2018, from www.unodc.org/unodc/en/human-Trafficking/Human-Trafficking.html

Welsh, J. (2009). *"It was like burning in Hell": A comparative exploration of acid attack violence* (Doctoral dissertation, The University of North Carolina at Chapel Hill). http://cgi.unc.edu/research/carolina-papers/health-papers.html

World Health Organization (WHO). (2013). *Global and regional estimates of violence against women: Prevalence and health effects of intimate partner violence and non-partner sexual violence*. Author.

2   Flesh Trading

Network of Organised Crime of Trafficking in Women and Minor Girls in West Bengal

Introduction to Trafficking in Women

Today's world is gravitating towards one of the most decisive forms of atrocities, that is, 'Human Trafficking.' Even after the twenty-first century, the world could not be free from this problem. In the past decade, such atrocities have fluttered to such an extent that they have become the world's third-largest form of 'transnational organised crime' after firearms and drugs (Darshna et al., 2016). According to the United Nations Office on Drugs and Crime (UNODC, 2012a), human trafficking is referred to as an act of recruiting, transporting, harbouring, or receiving a person through the use of force, coercion, or other means for the purpose of exploiting them. Such organised crime typically involves long-term exploitation for enormous economic gain. Yet men are also victimised, but most of the trafficked victims are women and children (Miko & Park, 2001). As per the official fact sheet released by the US Department of State on the issue of trafficking in women and girls, worldwide, more than one million women and children are trafficked every year for domestic servitude, forced labour, and sexual exploitation (Senior Coordinator for International Women's Issues, 1998). According to the 2012 UNODC report, sexual maltreatment is the most widespread form of trafficking, and among all the detected victims of trafficking from 2007 to 2010, sexual exploitation accounted for 57–62% (UNODC, 2012b). Each year, thousands of young women across the world are allured, abducted, or sold into forced prostitution and involuntary marriage. Kidnapping and abduction of women and children and child marriage are the popular methods of human trafficking adopted by the traffickers in recent days. Marriage appears to be an easy instrument for trafficking women to faraway places and exploiting them sexually and economically. It involved the gross humiliation of human rights across the world. A substantial body of newspaper reporting, as well as police reports and NGOs reports working on preventing trafficking, indicate that such activities not only happen in underdeveloped countries like India, Nepal, Bangladesh, and other Commonwealth of Independent States (CIS) but also extend into developed countries across the world, including the United

DOI: 10.4324/9781032696058-2

States. This indicates the complex, organised nature of this crime. The universal problem of trafficking may result from a constellation of factors that are broadly categorised into two parts. One is 'push factors' and the other is 'pull factors.' Most often, women belonging to remote villages with fewer facilities are being trafficked, believing the availability of a better lifestyle in outer places. High levels of poverty, adverse socio-economic conditions, illiteracy among women, lack of skills and income opportunities for women and their family members in rural areas, lack of awareness, pressure to collect money for dowry leads to sending daughters to distant places for work, a high level of disorganised environment, dysfunctional family life, torture by husband or his relatives, and many other related factors act as 'push factors' that lure them to go far away from their native place for a better lifestyle and job opportunities. Sometimes, geographically disadvantageous positions, natural calamities, war, epidemics, and so on act as push factors that make a person vulnerable to trafficking. As opposed to 'push factors,' there are some 'pull factors' like better access in big cities, lucrative job prospects, an easy way to earn money, the promise of better payments and a secure life by trafficking touts and agents, the demand for young girls for marriage in other places, the need for young women in the fast-growing prostitution industry, and the demand for young girls to avoid chronic diseases like HIV/AIDS. These pull factors act as lubricants and enhance the activities of trafficking. Despite these factors, improper patrolling systems, a lack of rigorousness in legal mechanisms, the unwillingness of victims and their families to seek legal redress due to a general fear of police, and the absence of support from neighbours persuade the culprits to engage in such criminal activities. It is a global health issue, overwhelmingly harming individual victims and transmitting diseases like HIV/AIDS (Miller, 2006). The safety and security of a country is also a great concern, as the profit generated by such organised crime networks has no respect for the rules and regulations of law and order. So, such modern enslavement of human trafficking is now increasingly under the limelight in the present-day context.

Present Study

Among the Asian countries, India is considered the hub of human trafficking. According to the US Department of State report on trafficking in person (USDOS, 2010), India is one of the major sources, destinations, and transit countries for trafficking. India is now placed on the Tier 2 watch list (Figure 2.1), more specifically known as the 'special watch list' as such inhumane activities are considerably higher and India is incapable of combating this situation (USDOS, 2018). In India, the state of West Bengal serves as a major hub of national and international trafficking of women and minors. As per the NCRB report, in 2016, out of a total 8,132 reported cases of trafficking in India, West Bengal reported the highest with 3,579 cases, which accounts for 44.01% of the national total (NCRB, 2016). Trafficking of poor women

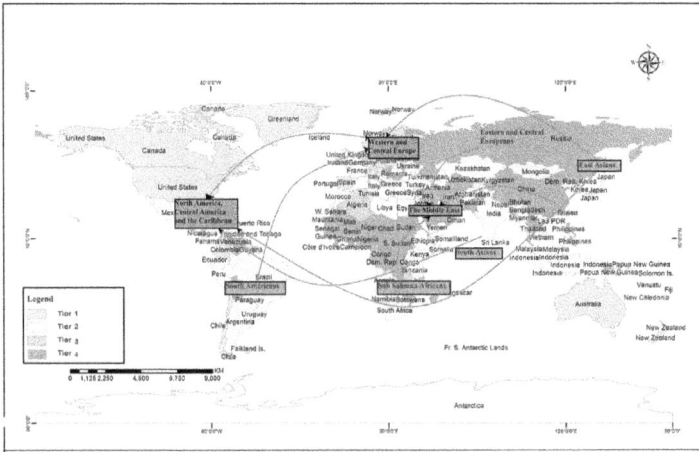

Figure 2.1 Trafficking in Person Report 2017: Worldwide Tier Placement and Flows of Trafficking

Source: US Department of States

and minor girls for commercial sexual exploitation (CSE) and gaining a huge profit from it is quite common in West Bengal, which has seen a gradual rising trend since the last few decades. As per the NCRB report, during 2016, there were a total of 3,569 female victims of trafficking in West Bengal, with 75.29% being minors, and of the 2,323 rescued victims, 78.30% were aged below 18 (NCRB, 2016). Incidences of kidnapping and abduction of women and minor girls (Sec. 363–369 IPC) in West Bengal are also very high. According to the NCRB report, from 2000 to 2016, there has been an ever-increasing trend of reported incidences under Sec. 363–369 IPC in West Bengal: 749 cases reported in 2000 to 4,976 in 2014, and it was slightly decreased during 2016 (4,494 cases) (Figure 2.2). It is also surprising that during 2016, a total of 3,14,674 females were reported missing in India, of which 53,654 were from West Bengal (NCRB, 2016). Moreover, 39,124 remain untraced in West Bengal. According to Atindra Nath Das, the regional director of a renowned NGO named CRY (Child Rights and You), it is important to consider the close linkage between missing children and organised crime. In West Bengal, another noteworthy incidence is underage marriage. According to the National Family Health Survey (NFHS-4, 2015-16) report, the percentage of under-18 marriages of women in West Bengal is 40.7%, which is a decrease of 12.6% compared to the NFHS-3 report (53.3%) carried out in 2005–2006. Child marriage is one of the most useful tactics used by traffickers to traffic minor girls, and most of the time, it remains secretive and hard to measure. All these phenomena are somehow associated with the trafficking of women in many ways.

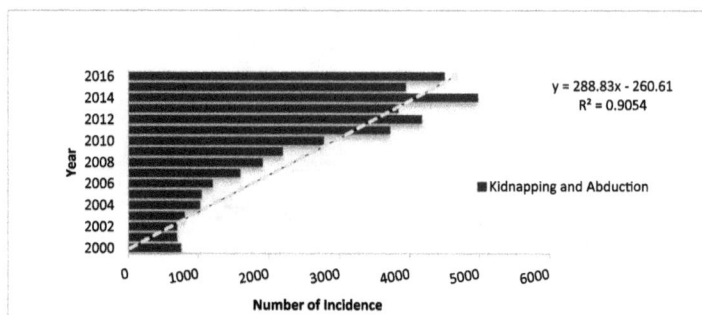

Figure 2.2 Incidence of Kidnapping and Abduction of Women (Sec. 363–369 IPC) in West Bengal from 2000–2016

Source: NCRB Report

Spatial Differentiation and Trafficking in West Bengal

From the existing literature, newspaper reports, government reports, and several NGO reports, in West Bengal, a complete spatial differentiation has been noticed regarding trafficking patterns and the factors that amplify insecurities among women and minor girls. In North Bengal, the intensity of trafficking is very much high in the tea garden areas of Darjeeling Himalayas, Dooars in Jalpaiguri, and Alipurduar (Ghosh, 2013; Yengkhom, 2013; Chhetri & Rai, 2015). The adverse socio-economic condition, lack of basic amenities, and geographically disadvantageous location (shares of porous national and international borders; inaccessible mountainous areas in Darjeeling Himalayas) induced the poor, uneducated, tea garden labourers to send their daughters to metros for better earning and thus trap them into trafficking (Ghosh & Kar, 2008; Bhutia, 2014). Contrary to North Bengal, the intensity of trafficking is very much high in the remote riverine villages of the deltaic Sundarbans of South-24 Parganas for its strategic geographical location, adverse socio-economic status, lack of basic amenities, frequent climate change–related hazardous situations and resulting vulnerabilities, and so on (UNICEF, 2005; District Human Development Report (South-24-Parganas), 2009; Ganguly, 2016; Molinari, 2017). The young women and minor girls from the poor families of the deltaic Sundarbans region migrate to metros under the pretext of dowry-free marriage, fake love proposals, domestic servitude, and dreams of a prosperous life, only to finally find themselves in the dark world, wherefrom it is hard to escape. Besides, illegal immigration through porous international borders, low levels of socio-economic status, threats of high level of poverty situations, and a lack of education among people make border districts like North-24 Parganas, Malda, Murshidabad, Nadia, North and South Dinajpur, and Cooch Behar an important source as well as transit areas for women trafficking (Dixit, 2017). In addition, studies also reveal that the industrial belt of Bardhaman district, namely Durgapur, Asansol, and Kulti, serves as major destination hubs as well as outflow centres of women trafficking (Ghosh & Kar, 2008). Trafficked women and minor girls from different source areas of West Bengal and neighbouring states Bihar and Uttar Pradesh are primarily brought to the industrial areas, wherefrom they are trafficked to several destination cities based on demand and rates (Ghosh & Kar, 2008). Besides these, the metropolitan cities of Kolkata and Howrah in West Bengal serve as major sources of transit as well as destination areas for women trafficking. Thus, in view of the existing scenario and underlying situational backcloths of trafficking in women and minor girls in West Bengal, the entire state can be categorised into three major zones: (1) trafficking in the Himalayan Region (Darjeeling Himalayas); (2) trafficking in the Sundarbans Deltaic Region (southern part of West Bengal, specifically South-24 Parganas); and (3) trafficking in plain lands and border districts (Kolkata, Howrah, Bardhaman, Nadia, North-24 Parganas, Murshidabad, Malda, North and South Dinajpur, Cooch Behar, and Jalpaiguri).

Aims of This Chapter

In this chapter, a case study has been done in the deltaic region of the Sundarbans of South-24 Parganas, considering distinct socio-economic and physical environmental settings to gain an insightful understanding of the magnitude of women trafficking, identify the trafficking hotspots, exhume the underlying situational factors that shape women's susceptibility, excavate the trafficking route map, and recommend some situational preventive measures to curb such inhumane practices in this region.

Case Study 1: Trafficking in Women and Minor Girls in South-24 Parganas with Special Reference to the Deltaic Region of the Sundarbans

Trafficking: A Great Threat in South-24 Parganas

'*Human trafficking*,' the most heart-rending bestiality against the human being, has been thriving in a terrific way in the district of South-24 Parganas for the last few decades. These notorious atrocities largely manifested against poor young women and minor girls in this district in the name of CSE, sex slavery, forced labour, and other forms of physical and sexual abuse. UNICEF has already marked South-24 Parganas district as an 'endemic area of child and women trafficking' (UNICEF, 2005). As per district-wise open government data (data.gov.in) released by the Ministry of Home Affairs, in 2015 South-24 Parganas ranked second after North-24 Parganas in terms of crime against women (Figures 2.3). Data also reflects that during 2002–2015, this district has experienced a growing number of incidences of kidnapping and abduction of girls and women in West Bengal after North-24 Parganas (data.gov.in). In addition, each year many women and girls remain missing from this district. According to an article published in a well-circulated newspaper *The Hindu*, South-24 Parganas is the leading district regarding reported incidences of missing children in West Bengal (Singh, 2018). In 2012, total missing children were 2,836, of which 2,191 were girls aged between 14 and 18. Only 1,007 missing children were traced (Singh, 2018). So, the question arises: Where have the remaining children gone? Yet the precise figures of missing, kidnapping, abduction, and trafficking of girls and women are unavailable to establish a concrete picture of the trafficking scenario in South-24 Parganas district, although daily newspapers have highlighted so many incidences of women trafficking happening in this district. 'SANLAAP,' a renowned NGO rigorously working on rescue and rehabilitation of trafficked victims, has identified eight districts in West Bengal as the major source region of trafficking. South-24 Parganas has been recognised as one of the most vulnerable among them (District Human Development Report, South-24-Pargana, 2009). This entire district has been grouped into three regions based on developmental actions likely to have taken place: Region-I, consisting of those blocks nearer to the metropolitan city of Kolkata, has better access and improved infrastructural facilities. These blocks are Thakurpukur, Mahestala, Budge-Budge I, Budge-Budge II, Sonarpur, Bishnupr I, and Bishnupur II. Region-II incorporates the north-west and mid-west parts of the district, including Baruipur, Bhangar I, Bhangar II, Falta, Diamond Harbour I and II, Mograhat I and II, Kulpi, and Mandirbazar blocks. Region-III covers the 13 riverine poverty-stricken blocks of the Sundarbans in the extreme southern part of the district. These blocks are Canning I and II, Basanti, Gosaba, Joynagar I and II, Mathurapur I and II, Kultali, Patharpatima, Kakdwip, Namkhana, and Sagar. Newspaper reports, NGOs, and several studies reveal that Region-III is more prone to trafficking. The locational disadvantageous positions of these riverine blocks of the Sundarbans and an intricate network of creeks make these regions isolated from the rest of the civilisation. Apart from the physiographic disadvantageous settings, this region is constantly affected by frequent climate change. The threat of tropical cyclones, monsoons, sea-level rises, and consequent floods and other natural hazardous situations creates a wide swath between these riverine blocks and the mainland. This results in acute poverty and homelessness and forces people to migrate as 'Climate Refugees,' and these susceptibilities somehow boost the propensity for human trafficking (Ganguly, 2016). Widespread poverty, illiteracy, lack of skills, and abject socioeconomic conditions compel the wretched and deprived local people to migrate to economically well-off regions for better livelihood options. The traffickers take advantage of these worse situations and put the poor women and minor girls in the trap of trafficking. Also, these regions share a porous international border with the neighbouring country Bangladesh, which also arouses illegal immigration and helps the traffickers to commit such organised crime in a very convenient way.

Methodology

Techniques for Selection of Sampling Size and Data Collection Tools

To accumulate textured information about instances of trafficking activities in South-24 Parganas, especially in the remote areas, a comprehensive sample survey has been done. Canning I and II, Basanti, Gosaba, Patharpatima, Kakdwip, Namkhana, Joynagar I and II, Kakdwip, Diamond Harbour I and II, Mograhat I and II Community Development Blocks (CD Blocks) have been selected as sample sites for data collection, keeping in mind their convenient accessibility and also that preliminary information about trafficking activities in these areas is available. A stratified random sampling technique has been used to select the sample size of the population for the survey. To carve out an overwhelming portrait of the flesh trade in the study area and accumulate both quantitative and qualitative data about trafficking activities, in-depth interviews with 420 willing respondents from different age groups, sex, educational standards, and occupational circumstances have been done based on a pre-structured questionnaire schedule. Besides, a total of 40 focus group discussions (FGDs) have been conducted with different stakeholders like police, Block Development Officers (BDOs), Gram Panchayat Pradhan (chief of Panchayat), NGOs, *anganwadi* workers, and teachers. Only those participants have been considered who agreeably took part in the interview and shared their views and experiences. The questionnaire mainly consists of open-ended, prompted questions, as individual respondents have their own views and experiences. To determine the variables (say, factors) accountable for increasing vulnerability to trafficking, a closed-ended questionnaire was used. The focus is on collecting information about demographics, perception studies, information on missing girls and women, reasons for being missing, problems associated with frequent climatic disturbances and related women's susceptibility, the economic condition of families residing in the study areas, whether any awareness initiatives have been undertaken by any government or non-governmental institutions, knowledge of legal aid, and so on. Above all, field observations have been done which reflect the socio-economic and physical environmental settings that stimulate organised criminal activities in this region. The information obtained from the questionnaire survey and FGDs has been further used to weigh up the trafficking attributes.

Methods

In this study, multiple methods have been applied to achieve the study objectives. To conduct this study, both qualitative and quantitative databases have been used. The fact-finding interviews and FGDs conducted with the willing respondents and case studies have been used as primary data sources, and the NCRB report, open government data (data.gov.in), the District Human Development Report (DHDR), NGO records, and the most circulated newspaper reports (*The Times of India, Anandabazar Patrika*) from 2015 to 2018 have been used as secondary data sources. After the collection of both qualitative and quantitative data, these were tabulated and analysed using MS-Excel. The quantitative information gathered from various secondary data sources and the perception studies of the local people and the focus groups helps to make a clear picture about the magnitude and spatial extent of women trafficking in the remote villages of South-24 Parganas. Thereafter, kernel density has been performed with the help of ARC-GIS 10.1 software to demarcate the trafficking hotspots in this district based on published newspaper reports on trafficking incidences. To excavate the most noteworthy factors that exacerbate susceptibility to trafficking, factor analysis (FA) has been conducted. By reviewing the existing literature, published and unpublished reports, and newspaper reports, several socio-economic and environmental factors have emerged that are responsible for intensifying insecurities among women and increasing the propensity to trafficking. So far, the researcher has prepared a structured questionnaire containing a total of 61 closed-ended questions (variables) under some possible determinants to determine the most responsible factors of women trafficking in this study area. These questions are subjected to the focus group participants ($N = 227$) and are instructed to give weight with respect to all the questions (or items) regarding the determinants of trafficking on a five-point Likert scale (Likert, 1932) ('strongly disagree'= '1' to 'strongly agree'= '5'). Thereafter, the internal consistency and reliability of the variables have been checked in all subscale dimensions by performing Cronbach's alpha reliability test (Cronbach, 1951). Then, exploratory factor analysis (EFA) has been run using extraction methods of principal component analysis to assess the underlying factor structure, which explains maximum variables in the best possible way (here it is to mention that EFA is used to determine the factor structure for a set of variables [or items] when minimal quantitative studies have been done regarding a measure) (Bandalos & Finney, 2010). The KMO (Kaiser–Meyer–Olkin) and Bartlett's test of sphericity results have been checked to test the eligibility of the data by measuring the sample adequacy for each of the variables. Thereafter, the mean score has been calculated to evaluate the satisfaction level of the focus group respondents regarding the factors extracted from EFA. SPSS 20 version software has been used to do all the statistics. Next, by analysing the primary and secondary databases, the researcher tried to excavate the potential domestic and international trafficking routes that are frequently used by the traffickers in South-24 Parganas. After that, a micro-level evaluation of the effectiveness of anti-trafficking measures has been done based on secondary databases and information gathered from direct intervention with law enforcement officials, NGOs, and other stakeholders. Finally, some strategic recommended measures have been provided that would help the government to take better initiatives to address such organised criminal nuisance in this district in a proper way.

Critical Analysis

The following sections discuss in detail the magnitude of trafficking in the remote villages of South-24 Parganas, specifically in the vulnerable areas of the deltaic Sundarbans; the targeted age groups; the most significant determinants; and trafficking routeways.

Hotspots of Trafficking in South-24 Parganas

From the discussions with the local people, stakeholders, and survivors, a clear picture of the magnitude of women trafficking in the remote villages of South-24 Parganas district has emerged. Women in the remote villages of this district are not safe. Especially young women and minor girls are more prone to trafficking. Very often, the lovers, spouses, kin, and relatives sold the women and girls to the traffickers on the pretext of job and marriage. Child marriage is very much predominant in the remote riverine blocks of this district. Government and non-governmental organisations have undertaken many initiatives. Continuous awareness campaigns are conducted. Nevertheless, trafficking is

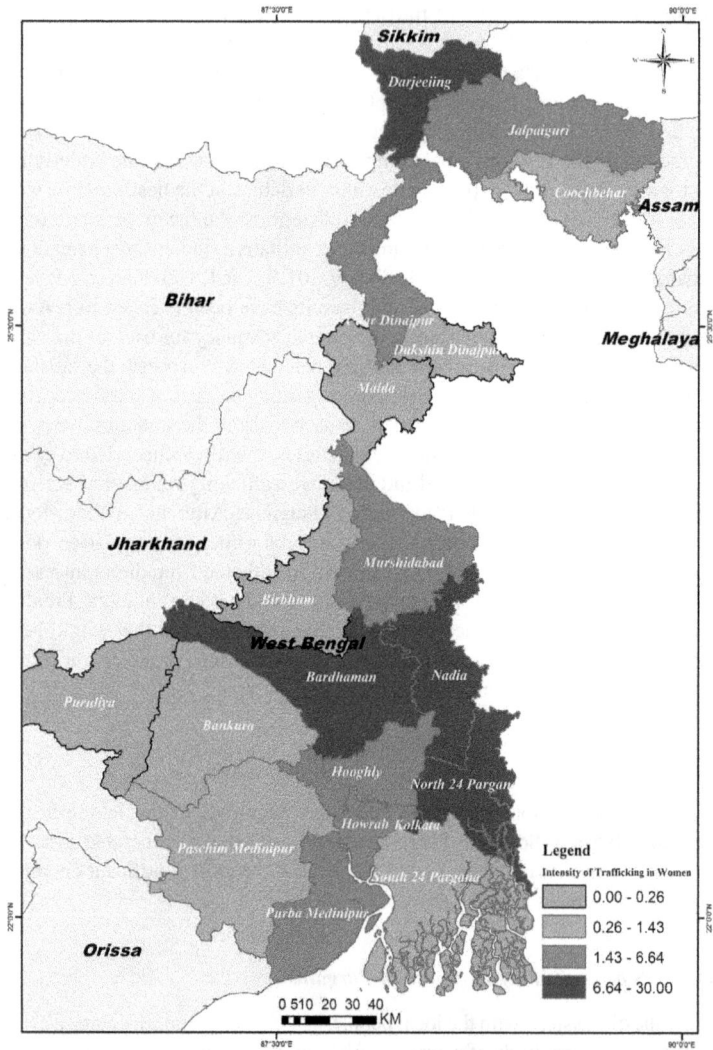

Figure 2.3 District-wise Incidences of Crime against Women in West Bengal during 2015

Source: data.gov.in

not completely eradicated. Figure 2.4 reflects the kernel density of trafficking incidences in South-24 Parganas based on some reports published in well-circulated newspapers (*Anandabazar Patrika, The Times of India, Ei-Samay*) from 2015 to 2018. This figure reveals that the remote areas of the Sundarbans deltaic region are the trafficking hotbeds of this district.

Trafficking Route Map: Flows of Trafficking in Deltaic Sundarbans

No fixed routes and patterns of trafficking exist in the deltaic Sundarbans region of South-24 Parganas, as trafficking is considered a complex organised crime that ranges from trafficking within one nation to cross-border trafficking. It appears from field surveys and FGDs that trafficking of young women and minors is very much rampant in this district, and the remote riverine villages of the deltaic Sundarbans are the most suitable source areas for such kinds of organised trade. For the fulfilment of basic requirements, aspiration for a modern lifestyle, and better earnings, the young women and minors from the remote villages of this district, like Enayet Nagar, Mandir bazar, Mathurapur, Joynagar, Taldi, Malikpur, Kultali, Kakdwip, Namkhana, Sagar, Canning, Gosaba, and Basanti, migrate to metros like Kolkata, Delhi, Mumbai, Chennai, Ahmadabad, Bangalore, Bihar, Pune, Haryana, Jaipur, and other small cities and towns holding the hands of *trafficking agents* (or say, *dalals*) who entice them by giving false promises of getting jobs in metros. Many of them migrate abroad, to countries such as Dubai, Malaysia, Singapore, and Saudi Arabia, and they finally get trafficked. Moreover, poor girls from Bangladesh are also brought illegally through porous international borders with the false promise of getting better jobs in metros. From FGDs, it has been portrait that to bring the Bangladeshi girls and women, the agents usually prefer to cross the river (natural boundary) near Hingalganj, North-24 Parganas district overnight with the help of *Dhur's* and kept them in the villages of Basanti, Gosaba, Canning CD Blocks of South-24 Parganas district for few days. Finally, the *dalals* sell them to the redlight areas, from where it is quite difficult for them to escape. Initially, the *dalals* bring the trafficked girls and women to nearby towns like Sonarpur and Baruipur of South-24 Parganas by roadways or railways. Thereafter, they are trafficked to the nearest metro cities of Howrah and Kolkata and forced to work as sex workers, strip dancers in hotel bars and pubs, beggars, or in domestic servitude, among other roles. Many of them are sold in India's largest redlight district, *Sonagachi*. In many cases, the agents bring the trafficked girls and women to nearby Howrah, Sealdah, and Bandel stations and handover them to other agents, who then bring them to destinations like Bihar, Delhi, Pune, Rajasthan, Ahmadabad, Bangalore, and Bhopal, especially in the brothels. Some are sent abroad also. Again, in many cases, the traffickers bring the poor girls and women from the

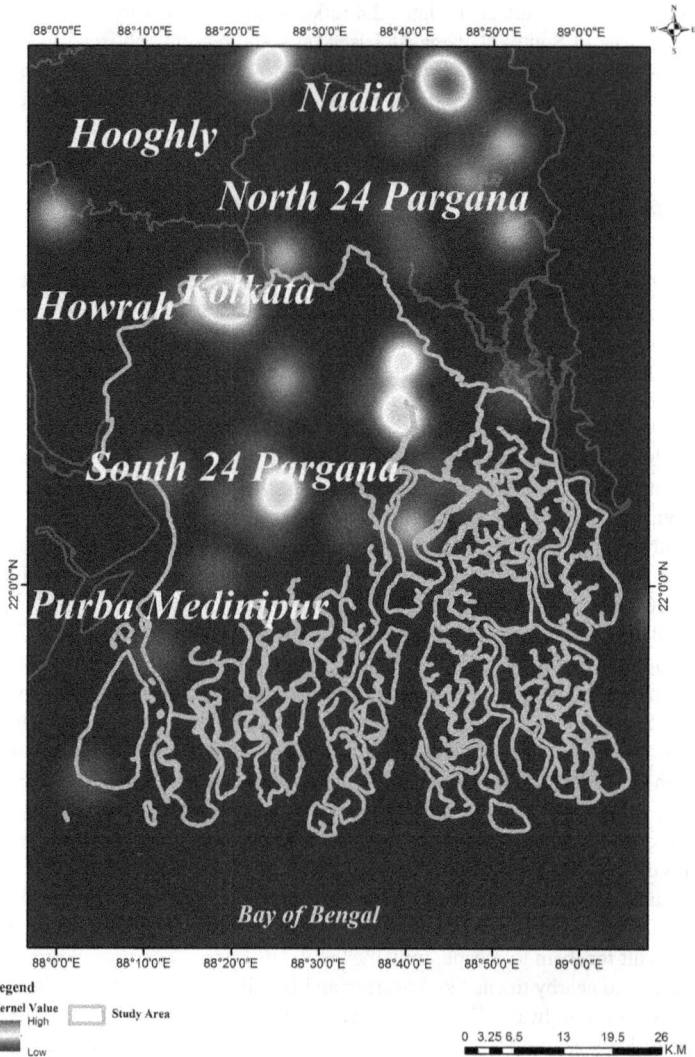

Figure 2.4 Trafficking Hotspots in South-24 Parganas

Source: Anandabazar Patrika, The Times of India, Ei-Samay

villages of Mograhat I and II CD Blocks to Haldia, Kanthi, and Digha towns of Purba Medinipur district, West Bengal, by crossing the Hooghly River and forcefully engaging them as strip dancers, bar singers, and commercial sex workers in hotels, bars, and redlight areas. From the FGDs, it is to be perceived that there has been a strong network of women trafficking, ranging from the South-24 Parganas to Kolkata and Purba Medinipur via Haldia. The agents use the roadways, railways, and even waterways to continue the trafficking rackets. However, the agents often alter their *modus operandi* to get rid of being arrested. In Appendix 1, some recent newspaper reports of women trafficking published in the well-circulated daily have been summarised. This appendix specifically illustrates the key source and destination sites of trafficking, which also support the opinion of the focus groups regarding the possible routes used by the traffickers in this region. The Sealdah railway station is considered one of the important suburban railway termini that connect the entire city hinterland with the metro cities of Howrah and Kolkata. The metropolitan city of Howrah is considered an important hub of transportation in West Bengal. It connects the entire North Bengal and South Bengal with the capital city of Kolkata by roadways and railways. It is well connected with the rest of India by railways and roadways. For such good connectivity, Howrah and Sealdah stations are frequently used by the traffickers to traffic the victims to distant places. Figure 2.5 illustrates the preferable route map used by the traffickers of this region. If the government could undertake potential initiatives following the concept of 'defensible space' (Newman, 1972) to lessen the easy escape opportunities of the offenders by enhancing proper surveillance on the above-mentioned preferable trafficking routes, the susceptibility of trafficking can be reduced.

Determinants of Trafficking in Deltaic Sundarbans

To excavate the most predominant risk factors that exacerbate susceptibilities and intensify the propensity of women trafficking in the study area, a structured questionnaire survey consisting of 61 questions (say, variables) regarding the determinants of human trafficking has been executed with 227 focus group respondents. The respondents were asked to give weight to each explanatory variable using a five-point Likert scale, ranging from 'strongly disagree' to 'strongly agree.' During data analysis, initially, the information collected from the questionnaire survey was screened, and inappropriate questionnaires were discarded. So, out of a total 227 responses, only 194 have been recognised as reliable, with a response rate of 85.46%. The reason for considering the rest of the responses (33 responses) as missed responses on the grounds of less reliability as per value is considered on a Likert scale. It was observed that the respondents did not respond to more than 15% of the questions (the threshold percentage outlined by Johnson (2003) for expulsion).

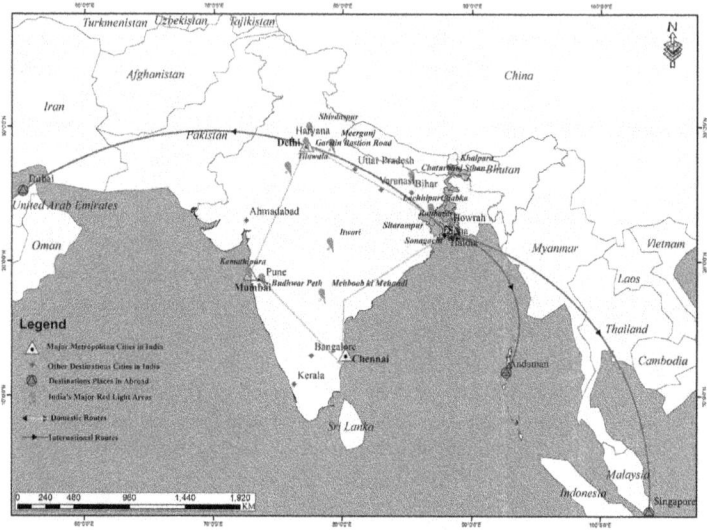

Figure 2.5 Flows of Trafficking from the Deltaic Region of Sundarbans, South-24
Parganas

There have been various recommendations regarding the minimum sample
size in factor analysis, namely 100 (Kline, 2014), 200 (Guilford, 1954), and
250 (Cattell, 1978). MacCallum et al. (1999) placed emphasis on consideration of the level of communality of the variables to determine the minimum
sample size. According to them, the desirable mean level of communality of
the variables should be at least 0.7. Henceforth, in this study, the sample size
population (N = 194) seems to be appropriate because the communalities of
all the 61 determinant variables ranged from 0.63 to 0.98. The mean level of
communalities was M = 0.88, except for four (0.59, 0.60, 0.57, and 0.56). The
resulting Cronbach's alpha value for each level is greater than 0.7 and supports acceptable levels of internal consistency within the variables (Appendix
2). (Note that Cronbach's alpha coefficient value of 0.70 or higher is considered 'acceptable' in most of the social science research work.) The overall
alpha coefficient value is 0.987, which also indicates strong internal consistency and reliability in the variables. The resulting KMO (Kaiser–Meyer–
Olkin measure of sampling adequacy) value is 0.856, and the Bartlett's test
of sphericity result (taking 95% level of significance, α = 0.05) with p-value
(sig.) of 0.000 is less than 0.05. Also, the approximate chi-square value of
31,925.339 with a high degree of freedom (df) rejects the null hypothesis (H_0)
(i.e., r = 0) and accepts the alternative hypothesis (H_1) that a significant correlation has existed between the variables. Therefore, it clearly specifies that

factor analysis is the appropriate method for further analysis of the datasets. In this study, we conducted Exploratory Factor Analysis (EFA) to comprehend the underlying factor structure of the responses we received on specific questions or variables related to the determinants of human trafficking. Appendix 2 also presents the factor loadings of the observed variables (the items/questions) after varimax rotation with Kaiser normalisation resulting from EFA by using the extraction method of principal component analysis, which results in 61 variables (questions) grouped into 7 major factors, with eigenvalues greater than 1. These factors are named 'status of education,' 'poverty and unemployment,' 'environmentally vulnerable area,' 'lack of basic amenities,' 'sociopolitical backgrounds and influence of social media,' 'gender discrimination,' and 'national and international borders and migration,' respectively, after considering the relative intimacy of the correlated variables under each factor. The percentage of variance in Appendix 2 expresses the percentage of total variance explained by each factor, and it is also noted that these seven factors together explained 87.49% of the total variables.

The value of the mean score (Table 2.1) helps explore the satisfaction level among the respondents concerning the factors of trafficking in the study area. From this table, it is observed that though the initial factors, that is, the status of education, poverty, and unemployment, have explained maximum variables (19.54% and 18.71%, respectively), most of the respondents agreed that factor 7 (national and international borders and migration), factor 3 (environmentally vulnerable area), and factor 4 (lack of basic amenities) are the major responsible factors of human trafficking in this region.

Table 2.1 Mean Score

Determinants of Trafficking	N	Minimum	Maximum	Mean	Std. Deviation
Status of education	194	1.08	5.00	4.10	.78170
Poverty and unemployment	194	1.00	5.00	3.88	.81949
Environmentally vulnerable area	194	1.00	5.00	**4.15**	.84588
Lack of basic amenities	194	1.30	5.00	**4.14**	.62344
Sociopolitical background and influence of social media	194	1.00	5.00	4.06	.77437
Gender discrimination	194	1.00	5.00	3.94	.88692
National and international borders and migration	194	1.00	5.00	**4.22**	.80794
Valid *N* (list-wise)	194				

Source: Computed by author.

Evaluation of Anti-trafficking Measures

Initiatives Undertaken by South-24 Parganas District Police and NGOs

Despite the constitutional provisions in IPC and CrPC regarding human trafficking and many anti-trafficking measures like the Swayangsiddha Project, Awareness Campaigns, Inauguration of Women Police Stations, and online web portal to lodge FIR undertaken by the central and West Bengal state governments, it is still very difficult to address women trafficking from the remote villages of South-24 Parganas district. In the last three years (from July 2016 to June 2019), the 'Swayangsiddha' project has succeeded in reaching its aim to some extent in this district. The police and NGOs succeeded in preventing many incidences of women trafficking from the remote villages of this district; many innocent girls were rescued from the brothels in Mumbai, Pune, Delhi, Bihar, and other metro cities and towns throughout India; and many trafficking agents got arrested. Details of the execution of this project are given in Table 2.2. But the numbers look like the tip of the iceberg. From the field survey and core discussions with the police and NGOs, it is known that despite the existence of strong legislative provisions and continuous awareness programmes, trafficking in women continues in the backward areas of Mograhat, Diamond Harbour, Joynagar, Sonarpur, Baruipur, and the remote villages of Basanti, Gosaba, Kakdwip, Namkhana, and Sagar blocks of the Sundarbans delta. Day after day, many poor girls and women from the remote villages are going missing. In an article published in a renowned newspaper *The Hindu* dated August 4, 2018, the author Shiv Sahay Singh minutely highlights how the district of South-24 Parganas has become a major trafficking hub irrespective of strong legislative provisions, how the young girls and women are being trapped into trafficking and exploited, their struggle for getting compensation, and efforts for prevention (Singh, 2018). In this report, he excavates several case studies, social boycott, the practice of

Table 2.2 Details of the 'Swayangsiddha' Project in South-24 Parganas District

Target Schools	*1,077 Schools in Total 29 Blocks*
Succeed to reach schools	More than 500 school
Participated girls (estimated)	34,005
Participated boys (estimated)	18,441
Succeed to outreach the people	70,259
Number of traffickers arrested	More than 70
Succeed to prevent child marriage	More than 150

Source: West Bengal Police and Swayangsiddha Website (www.swayangsiddha.org/).

child marriage, issues related to delay in compensation, and so on, which reflect the severity of the problem of flesh trade that exists in this district. From January 2017 to July 2018, the NGO *Shakti Vahini* and police together have rescued a total of 101 women and girls from different corners of North India; among them, one-third (34) were from the South-24 Parganas only (Singh, 2018). As per the report, Canning and Diamond Harbour are the two subdivisions of the South-24 Parganas district with the highest number of migrated people and the highest instances of missing children and women trafficking (Singh, 2018). During FGDs, the police and NGOs revealed that they receive information about numerous instances of trafficking during school campaigns. The 'Swayangsiddha' groups play a great role in those cases.

Rehabilitation and Compensation Scenarios0

There are several success stories where the South-24 Parganas district police have succeeded in preventing women trafficking. They successfully rescued many poor girls and women. But the problem lies with the issue of rehabilitation for the rescued victims. The lacuna of proper implementation of the 'Victim Rehabilitation Scheme' of 2017 (as a fundamental right under Article 21 of the Indian Constitution) is the main reason behind it. After being rescued from the dark world and brought back home, society blames them for their misfortune. Many times, due to attached social stigmas and the fear of being isolated from society, their own families do not accept them. Sometimes it even becomes difficult for financially weak families to bear additional responsibilities, so they refuse to accept their daughters. As there is limited room in the government-affiliated rehabilitation centres, it becomes a great challenge for the government to arrange proper accommodation for all the rescued victims. Apart from this, the West Bengal state government, in collaboration with several NGOs and self-help groups (SHGs), has taken initiatives to arrange medical care and vocational training (e.g., tailoring, bag sewing, making handicrafts, pot painting, etc.) for the rescued victims as a part of rehabilitation. For that, the government introduced projects like 'Swabolombon' and 'Muktir Alo' where free-of-cost training is provided to the victims. But that is not enough to survive. In 2017, the state government set up the 'Victim Compensation Scheme' and prepared a list of compensation for the victims. Still, many of them do not get compensation in time. According to the State Legal Services Authority's (SALSA) report, in 2017 only a total of 46 rescued victims and in 2018 (up to March) only 31 rescued victims received compensation. But the matter that makes law enforcement officials worried is that the number of recipients is much lower compared to the total rescued victims. Besides, the problem arises with the identity crisis (having no identity proofs, especially for those who are the victims of cross-border trafficking) of the victims. As a result, the rescued victims fail to return to mainstream society, are unable to continue the court cases, fail to get proper medical care, are unable to live the minimum level of living, and are forced to return to the dark world due to acute starvation and lack of earning. So, the solution does not stand on the rescue operation alone. It needs proper rehabilitation for the rescued victims. Not only in the South-24 Parganas district but also across West Bengal, proper rehabilitation of the rescued traffic victims does not happen.

Recommended Measures

The UN Protocol initiates several provisions to prevent trafficking and prohibit re-victimisation by establishing policies, programmes, and other related measures. Although stakeholders of South-24 Parganas adhere to some of the UN Protocol rules, the existing physiographic and socio-economic vulnerable situations, inequalities, and prejudices are being coupled with the exploitation of the victim's circumstances by the explicators, which causes myriad impairments to the victims who face extreme contravention of human rights. So, strategies need to be more systematic and situational facts oriented. Here some recommended measures have been provided considering the situational environment of trafficking in South-24 Parganas, so the government could take additional measures to combat trafficking from this region. These are as follows:

i   Police personnel and NGOs conduct awareness programmes in schools, remote villages of the deltaic Sundarbans, and other vulnerable areas under all the subdivisions in South-24 Parganas by arranging seminars, workshops, street plays, and so on. But such awareness programmes should also be arranged in colleges. Moreover, more and more ground-level conversations need to be performed with the poor people, more specifically people living in remote Sundarbans villages, about trafficking activities. Also, consciousness about legal provisions needs to be generated in poor people so that they can be aware of their rights and thereby develop zero tolerance towards exploitations.

ii As porous borders play a significant role in illegal immigration and trafficking of women and minor girls in South-24 Parganas, the Border Security Force (BSF) and immigration officials at borders need to be more vigilant and build a good network with law enforcement agencies to combat trafficking.

iii Surveillance needs to be increased in the most vulnerable areas, like villages in Basanti, Canning, Gosaba, Sagar Islands, and Kakdwip CD blocks of the Sundarbans region.

iv The Sundarbans deltaic region of South-24 Parganas is more prone to climate change issues like frequent cyclones, tidal surges, sea-level rise, and floods. These situations do exacerbate unaided situations and intensify the adversity of women trafficking. Therefore, aftercare treatment and management initiatives (ensuring food security, rehabilitation, alternative livelihood generation, poverty alleviation) need to be adequate and more specifically focused on women's rights.

v   This study has identified several potential trafficking routes that traffickers typically prefer to use. So, following the concept of Newman's (1972) 'defensible space,' if it is possible to minimise the easy escape opportunities of the traffickers by increasing proper vigilance on the above-identified routes and terminal points (e.g., Sealdah station, Howrah station, Bandel station, river transportation routes near Diamond Harbour, etc.), then the propensity of trafficking might be reduced.

vi Initiatives need to be taken by rural self-help groups to form a Micro Credit Society in the remote villages which aim to provide financial support to rural women so that they can start small-scale industries at home, overcome acute poverty, and uplift their livelihood status.

vii The NGO Impulse introduces the 'Impulse Model' in collaboration with government departments, law enforcement agencies, civil society organisations, media, and other private institutions with the aim of creating a trafficking-free world. They introduce the 6 P's (Partnerships, Prevention, Protection, Policing, Press, and Prosecution) and 6 R's (Reporting, Rescue, Rehabilitation, Repatriation, Reintegration, and Recompensation), which are undertaken for the north-east region of India. This could be beneficial for South-24 Parganas as well.

References

Bandalos, D. L., & Finney, S. J. (2010). Exploratory and confirmatory factor analysis. In G. R. Hancock & R. O. Mueller (Eds.), *Quantitative methods in the social and behavioral sciences: A guide for researchers and reviewers*. Routledge.

Bhutia, D. (2014). Gender discrimination and human trafficking in Darjeeling district. *Human Rights International Research Journal, 2*(1), 208.

Cattell, R. B. (1978). Conducting a factor analytic research: Strategy and tactics. In *The scientific use of factor analysis in behavioral and life sciences* (pp. 493–537). Springer, Plenum Press.

Chhetri, K., & Rai, S. (2015). Women trafficking in Darjeeling and Dooars. *Scholars Journal of Arts, Humanities and Social Sciences, 3*(7A), 1156–1158.

Cronbach, L. J. (1951). Coefficient alpha and the internal structure of tests. *Psychometrika, 16*(3), 297–334. https://doi.org/10.1007/bf02310555

38   *Flesh Trading*

Darshna, S. S., & Khan, T. (2016). *Judicial colloquium on human trafficking.* Judicial Academy.

District Human Development Report South-24- Pargana. (2009). *Department of Planning, Statistics and Programme Monitoring, Government of West Bengal.* www.wbpspm.gov.in/HumanDevelopment/DHDR

Dixit, M. (2017). Cross-border trafficking of Bangladeshi girls. *Economic & Political Weekly, 52*(51), 27.

Ganguly, C. (2016, September 10). The lost of daughters of the Sundarbans, West Bengal – the source, transit, and destination of human trafficking. *Core Sector Communique.* Retrieved November 18, 2017, from www.corecommunique.com/lost-daughters-sunderbans-west-bengal-source-transit-destination-human-trafficking/

Ghosh, B. (2013). Child trafficking in the tea gardens of Jalpaiguri, West Bengal. In A. Singh, S. P. Singh, & S. K. Biswas (Eds.), *Gender violence in India-perspectives, issues and way forward* (pp. 250–262). Bal Vikas Prakashan Pvt. Ltd.

Ghosh, B., & Kar, A. M. (2008). Trafficking in women and children in West Bengal. *Socialist Perspective, 36*(1–2), 10–83.

Guilford, J. P. (1954). *Psychometric methods* (2nd ed.). McGraw-Hill.

Johnson, M. L. (2003). *Lose something? Ways to find your missing data* (Series 17-09). Houston Center for Quality of Care and Utilization Studies Professional Development.

Kline, P. (2014). *An easy guide to factor analysis.* Routledge.

Likert, R. (1932). A technique for the measurement of attitudes. *Archives of Psychology, 22*(140), 1–55.

MacCallum, R. C., Widaman, K. F., Zhang, S., & Hong, S. (1999). Sample size in factor analysis. *Psychological Methods, 4*(1), 84.

Miko, F. T., & Park, G. (2001, August 1). *Trafficking in women and children: The US and international response* (p. 55). Federal Publications.

Miller, J. R. (2006, February 15). Human trafficking and transnational organized crime. *U.S. Deferment of State.* https://2001-2009.state.gov/g/tip/rls/rm/62072.htm

Molinari, N. (2017). Intensifying Insecurities: The impact of climate change on vulnerability to human trafficking in the Indian Sundarbans. *Anti-Trafficking Review,* (8).

National Family Health Survey (NFHS-4). (2015–2016). *Ministry of health and family welfare.* Government of West Bengal.

NCRB. (2016). *Crime in India: Statistics-2016.* National Crime Records Bureau, Ministry of Home Affairs, Government of India. https://ncrb.gov.in/en

Newman, O. (1972). *Defensible space* (p. 264). Macmillan.

Open Government Data, Government of India. https://data.gov.in/

Senior Coordinator for International Women's Issues. (1998). Trafficking in women and girls – An International human rights violation: Fact Sheet, US

Department of State, Washington, DC. *Trends in Organized Crime*, *3*(4), 21–23.

Singh, S. S (2018, August 4). Life after rescue: In West Bengal's human trafficking hub. *The Hindu*. Retrieved June 12, 2019, from www.thehindu.com/news/national/life-after-rescue/article24596244.ece

UNICEF. (2005, August 31). *Note on child trafficking*. Paper distributed by the organiser in a seminar on Prevention of Child Marriage, Dowry and Trafficking in Women and Children, Organised by the Department of Social Welfare, Govt. of West Bengal at Kolkata.

United Nations Office on Drugs and Crime (UNODC). (2012a). *What is human trafficking?* www.unodc.org/unodc/en/human-trafficking/what-is-human-trafficking.html?ref=me

United Nations Office on Drugs and Crime (UNODC). (2012b). *Global report on trafficking in persons*. UNODC.

United States Department of State (USDOS). (2010). *Trafficking in persons report 2010*. U.S. Department of State. Retrieved March 29, 2018, from https://2009-2017.state.gov/j/tip/rls/tiprpt/2010/index.htm

United States Department of State (USDOS). (2018, June 28). *Trafficking in persons report – India*. U.S. Department of State. Retrieved March 14, 2020, from www.refworld.org/docid/5b3e0b1ea.html

Yengkhom, S. (2013, March 4). Trafficking of tribal girls: Sick gardens trigger exodus. *The Times of India* (Kolkata ed.). Retrieved March 15, 2019, from https://timesofindia.indiatimes.com/city/kolkata/trafficking-of-tribal-girls-sick-gardens-trigger-exodus/articleshow/18785350.cms

3   The Modern Revenge Strategy of Acid Attacks against Women in West Bengal

Spatial Extension and Underlying Socio-psychological Milieu

Introduction: Acid Attack, a Modern Revenge Strategy

The most dreadful form of hostility against the human body that has plagued the world for the last decade is acid attacks, formally renowned as 'Vitriolage' (Nair, 2014; Kuriakose et al., 2017; Byard, 2020). 'Acid attacks' refer to an act of throwing acid or likewise corrosive material on an individual with an illegitimate intention to 'disfigure, maim, torture or kill' (Patel, 2014; Kuriakose et al., 2017). It is kind of 'Intimate terrorism' as it involves the deliberate throwing of chemical substance onto another person with an aim to disfigure out of jealousy and/or revenge (Welsh, 2009; Vietnam, 2014). Such form of brutality is on a mountaineering altitude in recent days, and most often the perpetrators are men, and young women become the sufferers of such violence (Kuriakose et al., 2017; Kaur & Kumar, 2020). The advance research conducted by the United Nations International Children's Emergency Fund (UNICEF) revealed that acid attacks are a very burning issue around the world, and even children are becoming sufferers in many cases (Nair, 2014). A study conducted by the Avon Global Centre for Women and Justice in 2011 revealed that throughout the world, including the United States and Great Britain, acid attacks have become a major human rights violation issue (Kalantry & Getgen Kestenbaum, 2011). Such violence is frequently used to terrorise and subjugate women and girls in a swath of Asia, from Afghanistan through Cambodia (Kristof, 2008). However, as per the Asian Legal Resource Centre (ALRC, 2003), it is too difficult to illustrate the gravity and extension of this menace as many cases go unreported. In most cases, the perpetrators use harsh chemicals, namely sulfuric acid, nitric acid, hydrochloric acid, hydrofluoric acid, phosphoric acid, muriatic acid, carbolic acid, and so on, with an ill-intention of distorting the victims' faces, which appear to be fiercer than murder (Patel, 2014; Kuriakose et al., 2017). The perpetrators use acid as a weapon to punish the victims for spurning their suitor's love or marriage proposals or sexual advances, denying dowry, domestic fights, property-related disputes, and so on (Guerrero, 2013; Yeasmeen, 2015; Kaur & Kumar, 2020) and thus want to see the victims alive with the scar of enormous physical and

DOI: 10.4324/9781032696058-3

psychological pain for the rest of their lives. Exposure to strong corrosive substances can have dire consequences, such as severe burns that can lead to poisoning, severe injuries, and severe excruciating pain. The exothermic reactions of acid with organic substances, that is, the living cells of human skin, damage the cells immediately. A strong acidic substance melts human flesh and even bones and could lead to rigorous consequences like death due to sepsis or multiorgan failure (Byard, 2020). In addition, permanent or partial blindness, scarring, paralysis, pulmonary disorder, and severe psychological distress may also be the long-term effects of acid attacks. This attack not only makes a scar on women's identity and trims down self-esteem but also makes them socially isolated, resulting in extreme physical torment and mental strain (Lohray, 2013). The physical deformities and resulting disabilities, post-traumatic stress, anxiety, and depression often led the survivors to shun all social interactions and live as outcasts, sometimes forcing them to take the risky decision of ending their life by committing suicide (Heanue, 2019). Thus, the horrific physical appearance led the victims die a hundred deaths physically as well as psychologically during the rest of their life (Biswas & Das Chatterjee, 2021).

Factors Persuading Acid Attacks in India: Context and Understanding

The 226th report of the Law Commission of India (Report No. 226, July 2009, W.P.(Crl.) No. 129 of 2006) reveals that a specific sexual category dimension has been noticed in India with regard to acid violence. Mostly young women in the age group of 18–29 years (Kalantry & Kestenbaum, 2011) became the sufferer for spurning suitors, refusing marriage proposals or denying dowry, and so on (226th report, 2008). Menon and Vashishtha (2013) in their study mentioned that in Indian society, the most frequent ground of acid violence is 'rejection of love proposals.' The vindictive lovers never accept the refusal from women, as it humiliates their dignity, fame, and honour. Failure to meet the excessive monetary demand of in-law's house is another significant cause of acid attacks in Indian society, as revealed by existing studies (Menon & Vashishtha, 2013). Besides, marital disputes, land- or property-related disputes, revenge in-between families, and other forms of sadistic pleasures by hurting someone else are also responsible for such decisive violent behaviour against women in India (Menon & Vashishtha, 2013; Kalantry & Getgen Kestenbaum, 2011). Apart from these, unlike other South Asian nations, the easy and cheap availability of acid in the open market is the key reason for acid violence in Indian society (Nair, 2014; Ahmad, 2012). Acid is used by gold-making shops, heavy and light industries, battery companies, motor servicing agencies, computer part dealers, and so on. For such widespread uses, acid is easily available in open markets in India. Despite strict rules and regulations

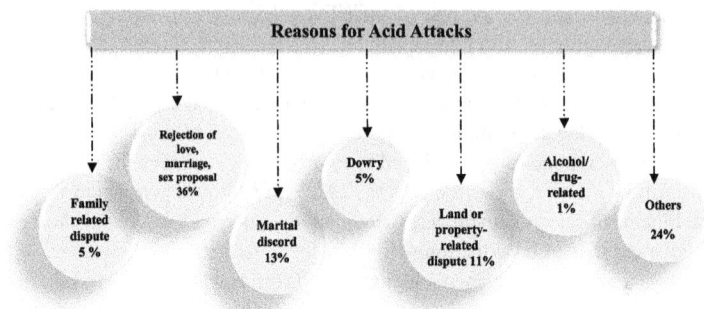

Figure 3.1 Factors Associated with Incidences of Acid Attacks

Source: ASFI report, 2017, Situational Analysis of Acid Violence in Eastern India

on the sale of acid in the open markets, no proper log to maintain the identity of buyers and details of the utilisation of acid is kept in shops and retailers. The Acid Survivors Foundation of India (ASFI) provides a strategic framework to delineate the causes of acid attacks in India (Figure 3.1) and reveals that about 11% of victims are unintentionally harmed just because they are nearer to them by chance (ASFI Report, 2017). The Avon Global Centre for Women and Justice in their report also accepts the fact that a substantial number of victims are not intended targets but are bruised as they are nearer to the targeted victims (Kalantry & Kestenbaum, 2011). So, it is the real time to think about such notorious atrocities and take tentative measures to prevent acid violence.

Present Study

Concerning the situation in West Bengal, acid throwing has become a modern revenge strategy against women in recent days. It is disheartening to watch news telecasts or read newspapers that are full of reports of the disfigurement of young lives with acid. In 2016, West Bengal held the foremost position in India, with 76 reported incidences of acid attacks against the human body (NCRB, 2016). Regarding cities in India, the state capital Kolkata (West Bengal) ranks second after Delhi (NCRB, 2016). Following the district-wise open government data (data.gov.in), it has been found that in 2014, the intensity of acid attacks against women in Bengal was relatively high in the districts of East Medinipur, Hugli, North-24 and South-24 Parganas, Bardhaman, and Uttar and Dakshin Dinajpur (Figure 3.2). This statistic also reveals that in South Bengal, prevalence is quite high in comparison to North Bengal. The analysis of statistics provided by NCRB illustrates that since 2010, incidences of acid attacks in West Bengal have been on an ever-rising trend: from 12 victims in 2010 to 83 victims in 2016 and the percent change in 2016 over 2015 is 94.87% in terms of incidences reported and 102.44% in terms of victims affected (Table 3.1). And if this continues in such a crucial way, it has been estimated that in 2023 the tentative figure will be 107 victims in West

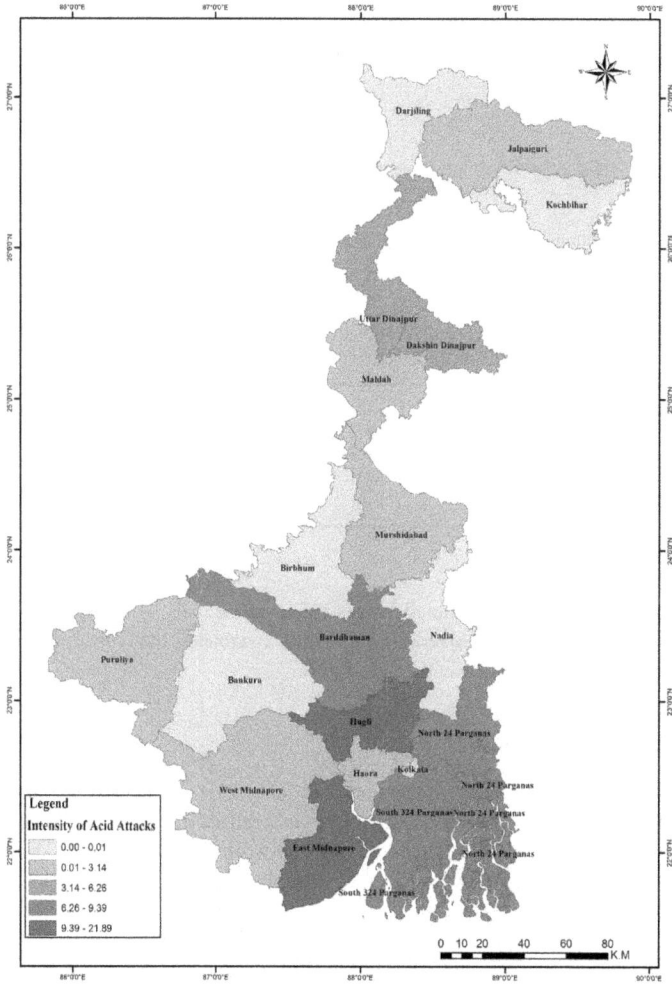

Figure 3.2 District-wise Spatial Expansion of Incidences of Acid Attacks against Women in West Bengal

Source: data.gov.in (2014)

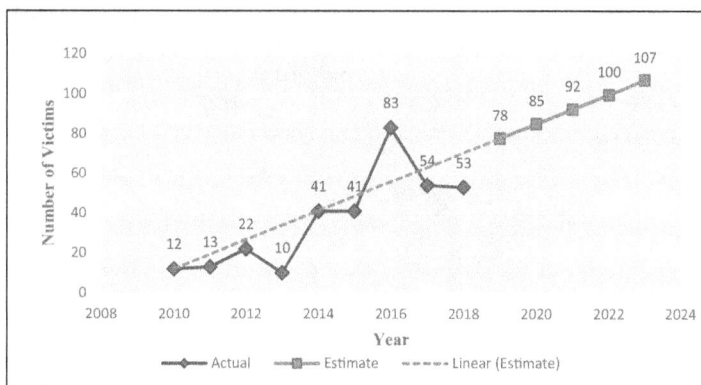

Figure 3.3 Future Trend of Incidences of Acid Attacks in West Bengal (2010–2023)

Source: NCRB Report (Author Computation)

Table 3.1 Tabulation of Incidences of Acid Attacks in West Bengal (2010–2016) and Percentage Change in 2016 over 2015

Year	2010	2011	2012	2013	2014	2015	2016	% Change in 2016 over 2015
No. of victims	12	13	22	10	41	41	**83**	**102.44**
No. of incidence	–	–	–	–	39	39	**76**	**94.872**

Source: NCRB report.

Bengal (Figure 3.3) (predicted values using MS Excel). It is expected that due to improved media coverage and human awareness, the reporting rate of incidences will be higher in the near future.

Aim of This Chapter

Several NGOs rigorously work to prevent acid violence and provide support and services like medical treatment, aftercare, rehabilitation, and legal aid to the survivors through building a channel network throughout India. As per the recommendation provided by ASFI's Kolkata-based area office, a weak judiciary and policing system, poverty, illiteracy, and gender discrimination are responsible for such horrible consequences in West Bengal. So, prior to the existing situation, this study intends to understand the magnitude and spatial extension of incidences of acid attacks in West Bengal; determine the most noteworthy socio-economic, psychological, as well as environmental factors that stimulate such notorious practice; recognise perception variations among the respondents regarding factors of acid violence; measure the effectiveness of existing legislative measures and provide a strategic situational crime prevention measure to minimise such inhumane practice enduringly.

It is thought that human behaviour is driven by certain traits that may vary from person to person based on their core beliefs, culture, and social environment (Nettle, 2009). As for culture, people undoubtedly rely on socially transmitted learned information and behave accordingly (Nettle, 2009). Hence, perceptions of criminological consent may differ from man to man according to their age, gender, occupation, socio-economic environment, and so on. Prior research on intimate partner violence (IPV) argues that no significant gender differences were found in IPV perpetration, but all concur that the factors contributing to such criminal acts differ by gender (Bethke & Dejoy, 1993; Nabors, 2010). Besides, people from varying age groups and varying occupational backgrounds have their own level of perceptions about criminogenic beliefs and attitudes. Most of the victims of acid attacks are younger-aged women (Patel, 2014). Thus, the views of that age group on the determinants of acid violence might be different from those of other age groups. Also, lawyers who directly deal with cases of acid attacks express their sole concern on the effectiveness of government rules and regulations on the sale of acid and confess that the easy availability of acid is the key determinant of such a brutal nuisance rather than other factors. Hence, some assumptions have been made based on the respondents' overview of the determinants of the acid attacks in West Bengal.

Hypothesis

H_{01}: Perceptions about the factors (dependent variable) of acid attacks do not vary significantly according to the gender (independent variable).

H_{02}: Age group–wise no significant variations have been found regarding the opinions on determinants of acid attacks against women in West Bengal.

H_{03}: There are occupation-wise no significant differences of opinions on factors of acid attacks.

Methodology

Techniques for Selection of Sampling Size and Data Collection Tools

The study populations included 210 respondents of varying age, sex, and occupational backgrounds. The general people, survivors, and their families, college-going female students, lawyers, and members of NGOs have been considered for in-depth interviews for this study. To select the sample-size populations, stratified random sampling techniques (Teddlie, 2007) have been solely adopted. Only those respondents were interviewed who willingly participated and shared their valuable opinions and experiences about this inhumane practice. The demographic profile of the study populations incorporates male respondents (51.90%) and female respondents (48.10%). About 52.39% of respondents (both males and females) were from the young age group (15–30 years). Yet perceptions of above 30 age groups have also been taken. Most respondents were college students (33.33%), and the rest of the respondents were unemployed males (20.95%), lawyers (17.14%), victims and their family members (9.52%), and NGOs (19.05%). About 73.81% of the respondents were graduates and/or educated at higher levels. About 33% of them were married, and 67% were unmarried. As literature reveals, young women are frequently targeted by attackers for rejection of love proposals and other sexual advances (Swanson, 2002; Kuriakose et al., 2017). So, the present study gives importance to understanding the perceptions of the young age group about acid attacks. At present, several NGOs rigorously work to combat acid violence. They provide medical care, counselling, legal and monetary assistance to the victims. So far, the present study has taken valuable information from the members of some NGOs that are working on acid victims throughout West Bengal. Statistics on acid attacks, the possible reasons, the health of victims, data on compensation, and so on were taken from the NGOs.

Methods

The present research study has been carried out in a very systematic way on the very emerging socio-psychopathological issues of acid attacks in West Bengal. Multiple methods have been applied to fulfil the study objectives. The situational analysis method has been used to provide sound information about the magnitude and spatial extent of incidences of acid attacks in this state. Both quantitative and qualitative datasets have been used to continue this study. The databases were collected from secondary data sources in quantitative form, such as the NCRB reports, Government of India (data.gov.in) reports, Kolkata-based NGO ASFI's records, and the most circulated newspaper reports (*The Times of India, Anandabazar Patrika*) from 2010 to 2017. Moreover, fact-finding interviews have been performed with some survivors and their family members; the general public, college-going female students, lawyers, and NGOs seem to be the primary data sources. The respondents were questioned regarding their perceptions about the rising incidences of acid attacks in West Bengal, the most targeted age groups, the possible reasons accountable for acid attacks, their feelings of insecurities, and so on. After the collection of both quantitative and qualitative information, these were tabulated and analysed using MS Excel. To determine the most noteworthy risk factors of acid attacks in West Bengal, factor analysis has been done. From existing literature, newspaper reports, and earlier studies, some socio-ecological factors have come to the fore that stimulate such criminal behaviour. To understand how much these factors are liable for rising the incidences of acid attacks against women in West Bengal, a structured questionnaire consisting of 19 questions or items under some possible factors have been prepared. These questions or items are subjected to the same number of respondents (210) and their opinions about the variables (say factors) have been gathered by the method of 'prefer by adding marks' (Osman et al., 2016). To gather their opinions, a five-point Likert scale (Likert, 1932) has been used. Cronbach's alpha reliability test (Cronbach, 1951) has been done for all subscale dimensions to check internal consistency and the reliability of the variables for further analysis (the value of Cronbach's alpha above 0.7 is considered to be adequate) (Nunnally, 1994). Thereafter, exploratory factor analysis (EFA) has been run using extraction methods of principal component analysis with varimax rotation (Anderson & Gerbing, 1988) to excavate the most significant key factors of acid attacks that explained maximum variables in the best possible way. Here it is worth mentioning that EFA, a data-driven technique, has been run instead of CFA (confirmatory factor analysis), as no existing theory or empirical study has been done regarding this issue (Suhr, 2006). KMO (Kaiser–Meyer–Olkin) and Bartlett's test of sphericity have been conducted to test data eligibility by measuring the sample adequacy for each variable. After the determination of factors, the mean score has been derived to measure the level of satisfaction among the respondents regarding the factors contributing to acid attacks. Thereafter, *t*-test and/or one-way ANOVA (analysis of variance) have been conducted with the key factors (dependent) and various demographic factors (independent) to justify the assumed hypothesis based on the number of categories of individual variables. Here, the variable 'Gender' has two categories: male and female. So, *t*-test has been performed. Again, 'Age' has four categories: 15–30 years male and female and 30–50 years male and female categories, for which ANOVA has been run. To understand the ANOVA result more accurately, the Robust Test of Equality of Means Welch Method has been used. To do all these statistics, SPSS 20 version software has been used. ARC GIS 10.1 software has been used to prepare crime mapping. To understand the socio-psychopathological trouble that the survivors face as the aftermath of acid attacks, a detailed analysis of the information gathered during direct interviews with the survivors, ASFI's coordinator Dibyaloke Rai Chaudhuri, and newspaper reports has been conducted. Finally, some strategic recommendations have been provided that would help the government take better policies to address such a heinous offence in a proper way.

Critical Analysis

Magnitude of Acid Attacks

From the situational analysis, a vivid understanding of the magnitude of acid attacks against women in West Bengal has been illustrated. The NCRB report revealed that during 2016, the total numbers of reported incidences and affected victims under Sec. 326A IPC and 326B IPC (women cases only) in West Bengal were 54 and 60, respectively (NCRB, 2016 Report). Data obtained from newspaper reports and ASFI records manifest that from 2010 to 2017, a total of 81 incidences of acid attacks in West Bengal have been published in print media (Appendix 3). By analysing this information, it has been found that during this time period, incidences occurred at a higher rate in West Bengal. The kernel density map (Figure 3.4) shows the major hotspots of incidences of acid attacks in West Bengal from 2010 to 2017 which specifies that especially the districts of South Bengal like North-24 Parganas, South-24 Parganas, Paschim Medinipur, Purba Medinipur, Hooghly, Bardhaman, Murshidabad, and Nadia have experienced the maximum percentage share of incidences of acid attacks during this time span. So, it has been observed that in the past few years, South Bengal has become the major hotspot of acid violence compared to districts of North Bengal. Another notable thing is that since 2014, the incidence of acid attacks in West Bengal has been on a rising trend, and more or less all the districts of South Bengal have witnessed such form of inhumane practice (Appendix 3). In 86% of cases (Table 3.2), women became the target of acid attacks by strangers, and about 14% of such inhumane practice happens against men. Against 81 incidences, the total number of victims was 106, out of which female victims were 81% and male victims were 19% (Table 3.2).

This analysis is based on female victims. The nature of acid attacks is typically represented in Table 3.3 derived from newspaper reports and ASFI records (from 2010 to 2017). From the situational analysis, it can be observed that the most vulnerable age group to acid violence were 11–30-year-old young women. In most cases, as they dare to refuse love proposals and disobey male strangers, they become the target of acid attacks. Yet there were so many incidences that occurred in West Bengal where middle- and older-aged women became the victims of acid violence. If the marital status of female victims has been considered, it is found that about 40% of victims were married, while 60% of victims were unmarried, divorced, or separated women.

As per newspaper reports and ASFI records, most of the incidences (about 42% incidences) of acid attacks occurred at night, especially at midnight, while the victims were asleep. The criminals choose this time to attack so that they can escape easily and the chances of being caught are less, although no specific temporal dimension of incidences of acid attacks has been noticed.

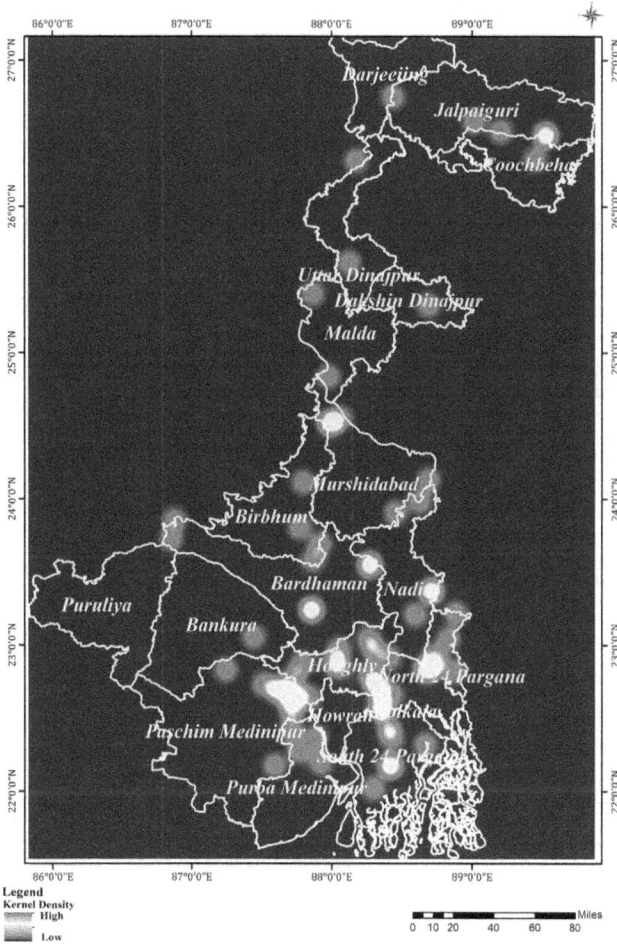

Figure 3.4 Magnitude of Acid Attacks against Women in West Bengal

Source: Newspaper Reports (Anandabazar Patrika and The Times of India) and ASFI Records (Modified after Biswas & Chatterjee, 2018)

Strangers used acid as a weapon to attack women to fulfil their revenge at any time throughout the day. It has been noticed that most incidences (56%) occurred at the victim's own residence. Yet, it happens outside of the victim's residence. It is also found that the most frequent acid used by the perpetrators was sulfuric acid. The inexpensive rate and easy availability of acid in the open markets help the offender do such illicit offences effortlessly.

Table 3.2 Summary of Incidences of Acid Attacks

Crime Head	Number of Incidences	%	Number of Victims	%
Acid Attack and Attempt to Acid Attack				
Female	**70**	**86.42**	86	**81.13**
Male	11	13.58	20	18.87
Total	**81**	100	**106**	100

Source: Newspaper reports (*The Times of India* and *Anandabazar Patrika*) and ASFI records.

Table 3.3 Nature of Acid Attacks

Vulnerable Age Group (As Per Number of Female Victims, N = 86)

Below 10 Years	11–20 Years	21–30 Years	31–40 Years	>40 Years
5	**36**	22	13	10

Marital status of victims (as per the number of female victims, $N = 86$)

Married	Unmarried
34 (40%)	**52 (60%)**

Time of occurrence (as per the number of incidences committed against female, $N = 70$)

Day	Noon	Evening	Night
20	9	18	**34**

Places of attacks (as per the number of incidences committed against female, $N = 70$)

At residence	Outside of residence
39	31

Type of acid used (as per the number of incidences committed against female, $N = 70$)

Sulfuric acid	Nitric acid	Muriatic acid	Carbolic acid	Not known
33	11	4	7	15

Source: Newspaper reports (*The Times of India* and *Anandabazar Patrika*) and ASFI records.

Factors Persuading Acid Attacks in West Bengal

From the existing studies, newspaper reports, and in-depth interviews with victims and their families, neighbours, victims' lawyers, members of NGOs, and law enforcement officials, many factors of acid attacks against women in West Bengal have been manifested. Factor analysis helps to identify the key determinants of acid attacks in Bengal. While analysing the surveyed informa-tion regarding factors of acid attacks, it has been noticed that 60 out of 210 responses were considered to be missed responses since their responses were quite inconsistent as per values considered on the Likert scale. Besides, the reliability of their responses was very less (<0.7), and they did not answer more than 15% of the items (questions), the threshold percentage outlined by

Johnson (2003) for expulsion. Only 150 responses have been considered reliable, with a response rate of 71%. The resulting Cronbach alpha value for each level is greater than 0.7, which indicates strong internal consistency within the variables (Appendix 6). The overall consistency is 0.879, which also indicates strong reliability in-between variables (Appendix 4). Henceforth, the sample size population (N = 150) in this study seems to be appropriate. The resulting KMO (Kaiser–Meyer–Olkin) value is 0.801 and Bartlett's test of sphericity result (taking 95% significance level, α = 0.05) with p-value (sig.) of 0.000 is <0.05 and also approximate chi-square is 5271.468 with 171 degree of freedom (df) accepting alternative hypothesis (H_1) that a strong correlation exists in-between variables (Appendix 5). Hence, it specifies that factor analysis is the right way for further analysis of the datasets. The factor loadings of variables (Appendix 6) after varimax rotation with Kaiser normalisation resulted from EFA (using the extraction method of principal component analysis) exhibit that all the 19 variables are clubbed into four major factors having eigenvalues greater than 1. These factors are rejection of love and marriage proposals; easy and cheap availability of acid in open markets; marital disputes, domestic violence, and/or dowry demand; and low educational standards. These four factors together explained 90.36% of the total variables.

Eigenvalues against each factor have been plotted in Figure 3.5. Here a sharp change in the curvature of the scree plot has been noticed after factor 4. It specifies that after factor 4, the total variance explained very less the remaining factors.

Hypothesis Testing

The resulting mean score (Table 3.4) expresses the satisfaction level among the respondents regarding the factors of acid attacks. It postulates that factor 1, that is, rejection of love and marriage proposal, explains maximum variables (28.41%), but most of the respondents considered that easy and cheap availability of acid in open markets and marital disputes, domestic violence, and/or dowry are highly responsible for rising the incidences of acid attack against women in West Bengal.

The result of the *t*-test has been given in Table 3.5, which shows that a significant difference (<0.05) exists among male and female perceptions related to factor 1 (rejection of love and marriage proposals) and factor 3 (marital disputes, domestic violence, and/or dowry demand) of acid attacks. Although the perceptions of both males and females concerning factors 2 and 4 (i.e., easy and cheap availability of acid and low educational standards, respectively) somehow matched, a slight variation is found in the mean score.

Age-wise perception variations among the respondents on factors of acid attacks in West Bengal are reflected through the result of ANOVA (Table 3.6). It signifies age-wise significance differences among male and female respondents (sig. <0.05) for factors 1 and 3; yet the mean score for these two factors is very

Table 3.4 Mean Score

Factors	N	Minimum	Maximum	Mean	Std. Deviation
Rejection of love and marriage proposal	150	1.50	4.50	3.1867	1.25406
Easy and cheap availability of acid in open market	150	1.40	5.00	**3.4360**	1.50580
Marital disputes, domestic violence, and/or dowry	150	1.20	4.80	**3.5893**	1.31625
Low educational standards	150	1.33	5.00	3.2556	1.32346
Valid *N* (list-wise)	150				

Source: Computed by author.

Table 3.5 Descriptive Analysis and Independent Samples *t*-test for H_{01}: Gender-wise Perception Variations Regarding Factors of Acid Attacks

Factors	Descriptive Statistics				t-*Test for Equality of Means*		
	Gender	N	Mean	Std. Deviation	t	df	Sig. (2-tailed)
Rejection of love and marriage proposal	Male	86	−.5550761	.98871949	−10.285	148	.000
	Female	64	.7458835	.24571111	−11.725	98.776	.000
Easy and cheap availability of acid in open market	Male	86	−.0403488	.98698557	−.572	148	.568
	Female	64	.0542186	1.02252339	−.569	133.192	.571
Marital disputes, domestic violence, and/ or dowry	Male	86	−.2676602	1.21093968	−3.985	148	.000
	Female	64	.3596683	.39676869	−4.491	108.254	.000
Low educational standards	Male	86	−.0073790	1.00512740	−.104	148	.917
	Female	64	.0099156	1.00091333	−.104	136.190	.917

Source: Computed by author.

low and lies close to zero. It indicates that though their perceptions about factors of acid attacks in Bengal are somewhat varying, it can be adjustable. The ANOVA result is also supported by the result of the Welch method (Table 3.7), although, no significant differences were found for factors 2 and 4 (sig. >0.05). It reflects the fact that all age groups irrespective of men and women concur that 'Easy and cheap availability of acid in open markets and 'low educational standards' are highly accountable for intensifying opportunities among the perpetrators to take revenge against women by attacking them with corrosive substances.

Occupation-wise perception variations among the respondents related to factors have been exhibited through the ANOVA result (Table 3.8). From

Table 3.6 Descriptive Analysis and ANOVA for H_{02}: Age-wise Perception Variations Related to Factors of Acid Attacks

Factor	Age	N	Mean	ANOVA	Sum of Squares	df	Mean Square	F	Sig.
			Descriptive			*ANOVA*			
Rejection of love and marriage proposal	15–30 years male	43	−.6357612	Between groups	62.679	3	20.893	35.338	.000
	30–50 years male	43	−.4743910						
	15–30 years female	34	.7607068	Within groups	86.321	146	.591		
	30–50 years female	30	.7290837	Total	149.000	149			
	Total	150	0E-7						
Easy and cheap availability of acid in open market	15–30 years male	43	−.0635466	Between groups	.381	3	.127	.125	.945
	30–50 years male	43	−.0171509						
	15–30 years female	34	.0445280	Within groups	148.619	146	1.018		
	30–50 years female	30	.0652014	Total	149.000	149			
	Total	150	0E-7						
Marital disputes, domestic violence, and/ or dowry	15–30 years male	43	−.4602644	Between groups	18.258	3	6.086	6.796	.000
	30–50 years male	43	−.0750559						
	15–30 years female	34	.2666436	Within groups	130.742	146	.895		
	30–50 years female	30	.4650964	Total	149.000	149			
	Total	150	0E-7						
Low educational standards	15–30 years male	43	−.1060461	Between groups	1.168	3	.389	.385	.764
	30–50 years male	43	.0912880						
	15–30 years female	34	−.0564840	Within groups	147.832	146			
	30–50 years female	30	.0851685	Total	149.000	149	1.013		
	Total	150	0E-7						

Source: Computed by author.

this, it is revealed that for factors 1, 3, and 4, perceptions between groups and within groups among the respondents vary significantly (sig. <0.05), yet not so much since the mean score lies near zero for all occupational groups. But no significant differences have been found for factor 2, that is, 'easy and cheap availability of acid in open markets' (sig. >0.05). More or less all the respondents quite concur with this harsh fact of acid attacks against women in West Bengal. Since variances among all factors are not equal, the Welch method has been applied to minimise the errors (Table 3.9). The Welch results

Table 3.7 Robust Tests of Equality of Means: Welch Method for H_{02}

Factor		Statistics[a]	df1	df2	Sig.
Rejection of love and marriage proposal	Welch	45.327	3	77.407	.000
Easy and cheap availability of acid in open market	Welch	.117	3	77.112	.950
Marital disputes, domestic violence, and/or dowry	Welch	10.200	3	76.312	.000
Low educational standards	Welch	.379	3	77.540	.768
a. Asymptotically F distributed					

Source: Computed by author.

Table 3.8 ANOVA Table for H_{03}: Occupation-wise Perception Variations concerning Factors of Acid Attacks

Factor		Sum of Squares	df	Mean Square	F	Sig.
Rejection of love and	Between groups	96.970	4	24.242	67.560	.000
marriage proposal	Within groups	52.030	145	.359		
	Total	149.000	149			
Easy and cheap	Between groups	3.529	4	.882	.879	.478
availability of acid	Within groups	145.471	145	1.003		
in open market	Total	149.000	149			
Marital disputes,	Between groups	32.587	4	8.147	10.147	.000
domestic violence,	Within groups	116.413	145	.803		
and/or dowry	Total	149.000	149			
Low educational	Between groups	9.087	4	2.272	2.354	.057
standards	Within groups	139.913	145	.965		
	Total	149.000	149			

Source: Computed by author.

Table 3.9 Robust Tests of Equality of Means: The Welch Method for H_{03}

Factor		Statistics[a]	df1	df2	Sig.
Rejection of love and marriage proposal	Welch	63.885	4	58.080	.000
Easy and cheap availability of acid in open market	Welch	.893	4	46.349	.476
Marital disputes, domestic violence, and/or dowry	Welch	16.754	4	51.948	.000
Low educational standards	Welch	3.336	4	47.941	.017
[a]Asymptotically *F* distributed.					

Source: Computed by author.

also validate the ANOVA result. In addition to these key issues obtained from the EFA, many other responsible factors for acid violence in West Bengal have been egressed from the opinion of the respondents. These are family disputes, land or property disputes, revenge, and so on.

Evaluation of Undertaken Measures and Suggestive Recommendations

In India, the violence of acid attacks has spread like a fire in recent days. Activists demand for limiting the sale of acidic substance in the open market by posing strict regulations as cheap availability of acid seems to be the key determinant of acid violence in India. Until 2013, there were no separate sections of acid attacks mentioned in the IPC as it did not consider a separate offence. Previously, this notorious offence was dealt under Section 326 IPC, which deals with 'Voluntarily causing grievous hurt by dangerous weapons or means and/or using corrosive substance.' After the brutal incidence of the '2012 Delhi Gang Rape case,' the Supreme Court of India ordered the parliament to straighten existing laws. Henceforth, in 2013, 'The Criminal Law (Amendment)' had been introduced headed by Justice A. R. Lakshmann. By virtue of this law, Sections 326-A and 326-B have been added in IPC which made acid attacks to be considered a specific crime under IPC. Although there are provisions mentioned under the IPC, many incidences go unreported due to unawareness and the withdrawal of the cases is also noticed because of repercussions from the offenders and their families. Data gathered from newspaper reports and ASFI records reflect that out of 70 reported incidences committed particularly against women in Bengal, the number of perpetrators was 85. In 71% of the cases, offenders are in police custody (Table 3.10), although the charge sheets are not prepared for many cases. In three cases, the court has sent the culprits for life imprisonment. For the Machlandapur acid attack case, North-24 Parganas was the first one where the Barasat court punished the accused for life imprisonment. For the Cooch Behar acid attack case (held in 2015), the Alipurduar additional district and session court has sentenced the culprits for life imprisonment. This is the first case in North Bengal where the perpetrator of an acid attack has been convicted and punished. For Mou Rajak case of Nadia, the Krishnanagar fast-track court punished the accused by sentencing him for life imprisonment. For Dipabali Rajak case of Baishnabnagar, Malda, and Dhanekhali case, the culprits were punished for ten years imprisonment with fine. It has also been reflected from the situational analysis that in about 14% of cases, the accused have not been arrested yet. In 7% of cases, the victims' family did not lodge an FIR (First Information Report) due to fear of reprisal from the perpetrators. Sometimes, it becomes very difficult for the victims to detect the offenders as the perpetrators come in motorbikes having covered their face with cloths and the person who sits on the back of the rider throw acid on victims' face and run away (Goswami, 2017).

Table 3.10 Legal Actions Undertaken for the Offenders in West Bengal

Legal Action	Numbers	Percentage
In police custody	50	**71.43**
10 years jail	2	2.86
Lifetime imprisonment	3	4.29
Not arrested	10	14.29
Not complained	5	7.14
Total incidence	70	100

Source: Newspaper report (*The Times of India* and *Anandabazar Patrika*) and ASFI records.

Besides, the Supreme Court of India, on July 18, 2013, for the first time, declared regulations (in the context of *Laxmi v. Union of India* case (W.P.[Crl.] No. 129/2006)) on the sale of acid and other corrosive substances in open markets (under 'The Poison Possession and Sale Rules, 2013,' Writ Petition order dated July 18, 2013), placing emphasis on the compensation to the victims and treatment of sufferers at no cost (Laxmi vs. Union of India, 2014). The Supreme Court also directed all states and UTs to take proper steps regarding the inclusion of survivors' names under the disability list (*Parivartan Kendra v. UOI* case 2015). But from 2010 to 2017 in West Bengal, only ten survivors got compensation from the government, although this was not enough for their treatment as they had to undergo many surgeries. A widow victim in Ghatal, in Paschim Medinipur district, died just after compensation was signed by the government for her treatment and aftercare. Despite the strict rules and regulations on the sale of acid and other corrosive substances, acid is easily available in the open markets in West Bengal. The Barabazar area of Kolkata is the main hub of acid in Bengal. The hardware retailers and battery retailers in Kolkata suburban buy acid from the wholesalers in Barabazar (Kolkata) and sell in the local markets. In Ghatal subdivision, Paschim Medinipur, Gaighata, Bongaon, Habra, Ashok Nagar, Bagda of North-24 Parganas, Gopal Nagar of Hooghly, Baishnabnagar of Malda, and many other places of Nadia and Murshidabad districts, acid is readily available in grocery stores, hardware shops, battery shops, and other local stores in town and villages. Some identified market areas in West Bengal where acid and other corrosive substances are readily available have been portrayed in Figure 3.5. Most of the people in the Ghatal subdivision are engaged in goldwork, for which acid is necessary. In Sagarpur area of the Daspur CD block, people are also engaged in the gold-making industry. It is so surprising that in most of the cases of acid attacks in the Ghatal subdivision area and adjacent CD blocks, the perpetrators are gold mechanics. On November 10, 2017, CID arrested a broker from Panuhat Barujibipally of Katowa subdivision, Burdwan, with 2,200 litres of acid. In March 2017, raids were conducted in Sonarpur and Baruipur market areas by law enforcement officials under the supervision

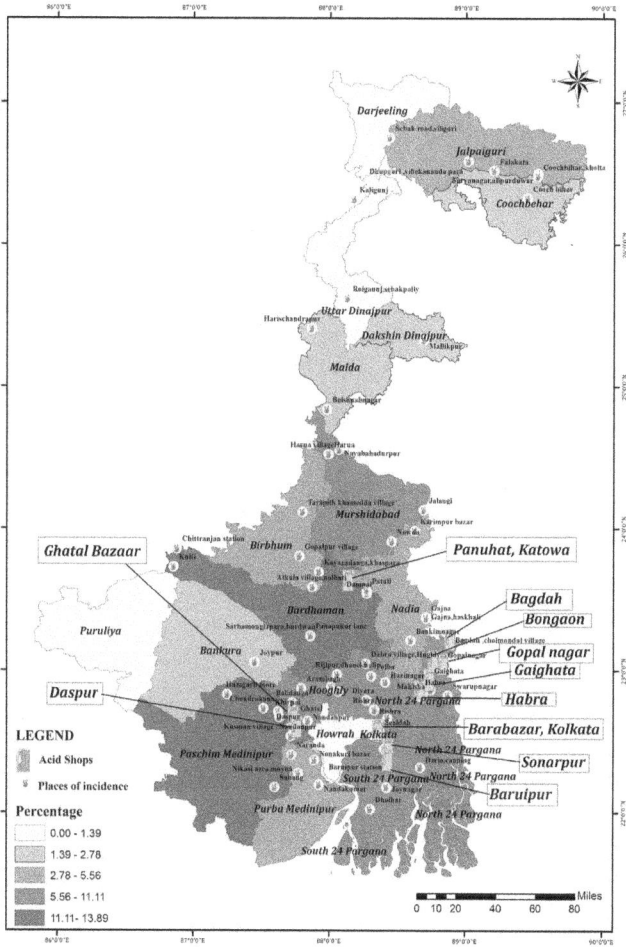

Figure 3.5 Sale of Acid in Open Markets: Some Identified Market Areas in West Bengal

Source: Newspaper reports, ASFI records, and field survey

of the Sub-Divisional Police Officer (SDPO) (Baruipur) and Sub-Divisional Magistrate (Baruipur) of South-24 Parganas district. It was so astonishing that the police seized numerous sulfuric acid and nitric acid bottles from the hardware shops in Baruipur and Sonarpur markets. A renowned police officer from South-24 Parganas district police also said that in 2017 around 200 litres of acid from a battery industry in the Rathtala area of Sonarpur subdivision were seized by police. There are many gold shops and heavy industries in

Bagnan, Uluberia subdivision of Howrah. Most of the retailers have no legal license. They only manage trade licences from the local panchayat or municipality for retailing acid in the open market. But a single drop of acid is enough to distort the human body. Hence, it can be observed that, notwithstanding the existence of strict government measures, ignorance of government rules is very much noticed in West Bengal.

So, the government needs to be strict enough to execute the laws and regulations and conduct rigorous monitoring on the counter-selling of acid, provide proper medical supports and compensations, make court procedures faster to punish the culprits, and make strong collaborations with NGOs and civil societies to make people aware of acid attacks. Here some suggestive measures have been recommended along with government initiatives considering the underlying situational environment in West Bengal to wipe out such inhumane practices from our society enduringly:

(1) Continuous surveillance is required on the sale of acid in the open markets. The identified market areas, namely Ghatal, Daspur (Paschim Medinipur), Sonarpur (South-24 Parganas), Purbasthali (Bardhaman), Gopal Nagar (Hooghly), Habra, Ashok Nagar, Gaighata, Bongaon (North-24 Parganas), Baishnabnagar (Malda), and so on, where acid is easily available in hand, should be under special vigilance.
(2) School-based initiatives are needed to make students aware of acid attacks so that they can take dynamic roles to advocate for the prevention of acid attacks among their communities.
(3) Making posters about such ghastly nuisance in public places, namely in the railway stations, police stations, bus stops, and other crowded areas. specifically in the most vulnerable districts, to make people aware of acid attacks.
(4) Initiatives need to be taken to disclose the identity of the perpetrators. Therefore, in every public place, photos of the perpetrators should be displayed.

These situational measures might be helpful to the government to combat acid attacks against women in West Bengal effectively, to provide special care to the survivors so that they can live in society with dignity and honour, and an acid attack–free society could be formed.

References

Ahmad, N. (2012). Weak laws against acid attacks on women: An Indian perspective. *Medico-Legal Journal, 80*(3), 110–120.

ALRC. (2003, March 10). *Integration of the human rights of women and the gender perspectives: Violence against women* (E/CN.4/2003/NGO/96). Economic and Social Council, United Nations. https://digitallibrary.un.org/record/491547?ln=es

Anderson, J. C., & Gerbing, D. W. (1988). Structural equation modeling in practice: A review and recommended two-step approach. *Psychological Bulletin, 103*(3), 411.

ASFI Report. (2017). *Situational analysis of acid violence in Eastern India.* Acid Survivors Foundation of India: Positive Prevention-Rebuilding Life.

Bethke, T. M., & DeJoy, D. M. (1993). An experimental study of factors influencing the acceptability of dating violence. *Journal of Interpersonal Violence, 8*(1), 36–51.

Biswas, P., & Chatterjee, N. D. (2018). Acid attacks: A threat against women-measure the effectiveness of existing legislatures to curb acid violence. *Eastern Geographer, XXIV*(1), 149–158.

Biswas, P., & Das Chatterjee, N. (2021). Factors persuading acid attacks, a modern revenge strategy against women: A study in West Bengal, India. *Indian Journal of Geography & Environment, 17–18*, 106–117.

Byard, R. W. (2020). The manifestations of acid attacks (vitriolage or vitriolism). *Forensic Science, Medicine and Pathology, 16*, 387–388.

Cronbach, L. J. (1951). Coefficient alpha and the internal structure of tests. *Psychometrika, 16*(3), 297–334.

Goswami, M. (2017). A review of literatures on acid attacks in India. *MSSV Journal of Humanities and Social Sciences, 1*(2), 1–10.

Guerrero, L. (2013). Burns due to acid assaults in Bogotá, Colombia. *Burns, 39*(5), 1018–1023.

Heanue, S. (2019). *Indian acid attacks are on the rise, and the women who survive them are forced to live as outcasts.* Retrieved December 29, 2019, from www. abc.net.au/news/2019-08-24/indian-acid-victims-want-to-break-down-social-stigma/11428952

Johnson, M. L. (2003). *Lose something? Ways to find your missing data* (Series 17-09). Houston Center for Quality of Care and Utilization Studies Professional Development.

Kalantry, S., & Getgen Kestenbaum, J. (2011). *Combating acid violence in Bangladesh, India and Cambodia.* Cornell Legal Studies Research Paper No. 11-24. http://dx.doi.org/10.2139/ssrn.1861218

Kaur, N., & Kumar, A. (2020). Vitriolage (vitriolism)-a medico-socio-legal review. *Forensic Science, Medicine and Pathology*, 1–8. https://doi.org/10.1007/s12024-020-00230-7.

Kristof, N. D. (2008). Video clip. *New York Times.* Retrieved December 11, 2017, from www.nytimes.com/video/opinion/1194834033797/acid-attacks.html

Kuriakose, F., Mallick, N., & Iyer, D. K. (2017). Acid violence in South Asia: A structural analysis toward transformative justice. *ANTYAJAA: Indian Journal of Women and Social Change, 2*(1), 65–80.

Law Commission of India. (2009, July). The inclusion of acid attacks to specific offence in the Indian Penal Code and Law for Victims of Crime, 3 (226th Report).

Laxmi vs. Union of India. (2014). 4 SCC 427. *NYAYA DEEP: The Official Journal of NALSA, XVII*(2).

Likert, R. (1932). A technique for the measurement of attitudes. *Archives of Psychology, 22*(140), 1–55.

Lohray, U. B. (2013). Criminalization of acid crimes and implementing the law in the South East Asian subcontinent. *Commonwealth Law Bulletin, 39*(4), 619–630.

Menon, P., & Vashishtha, S. (2013). Vitriolage & India – the modern weapon of revenge. *International Journal of Humanities and Social Science Invention, 2*(10), 1–9. www.ijhssi.org/papers/v2(10)/Version-2/A0210020109.pdf

Nabors, E. L. (2010). Drug use and intimate partner violence among college students: An in-depth exploration. *Journal of Interpersonal Violence, 25*(6), 1043–1063.

Nair, A. R. (2014). Acid attack-violence against women 'need of the hour'. *Journal of Innovative Research and Solution (JIRAS), 1*(1).

Nettle, D. (2009). Ecological influences on human behavioural diversity: A review of recent findings. *Trends in Ecology & Evolution, 24*(11), 618–624.

Nunnally, J. C. (1994). *Psychometric theory 3E*. Tata McGraw-Hill Education.

Osman, T., Divigalpitiya, P., & Arima, T. (2016). Driving factors of urban sprawl in Giza governorate of the Greater Cairo Metropolitan Region using a logistic regression model. *International Journal of Urban Sciences, 20*(2), 206–225.

Patel, M. (2014). A desire to disfigure: Acid attack in India. *International Journal of Criminology and Sociological Theory, 7*(2), 1–11.

Suhr, D. D. (2006). Exploratory or confirmatory factor analysis? *SUGI 31 Proceedings*, 1–17. https://doi.org/10.1002/da.20406.

Swanson, J. (2002). Acid attacks: Bangladesh's efforts to stop the violence. *Harvard Health Policy Review, 3*(1), 82–88.

Teddlie, C., & Yu, F. (2007). Mixed methods sampling: A typology with examples. *Journal of Mixed Methods Research, 1*(1), 77–100.

Welsh, J. (2009). *"It was like burning in Hell": A comparative exploration of acid attack violence* (Doctoral dissertation, The University of North Carolina at Chapel Hill). http://cgi.unc.edu/research/carolina-papers/health-papers.html

Yeasmeen, N. (2015). Acid attack in the back drop of India and Criminal Amendment Act, 2013. *International Journal of Humanities and Social Science Invention, 4*, 6–13.

Bibliography

Anandabazar Patrika. www.anandabazar.com/

Data.gov.in. Open Government Data, Government of India. https://data.gov.in/

National Crime Record Bureau, Ministry of Home Affairs, Govt. of India. http://ncrb.gov.in/

The Times of India. https://timesofindia.indiatimes.com/

4 Rape

Brutality against Women in West Bengal: A Geospatial Understanding

Introduction: Rape – Brutality against Women

In today's world, criminological studies give more attention to the very emerging criminal issue of rape, the most crucial form of sexual violence against women that restricts women's movements and put their lives at great risk. In the last few decades, such notorious criminal nuisance has become so deep-rooted in our society that safety of women has become a big question throughout the world. Not a day passes when news channels around the world do not telecast news about violence against women. A depressive mood develops while reading daily newspapers or seeing various news channels or surfing online news that are full of rape and other forms of sexual brutalities against women. The phrase 'Rape' against women is defined as forceful sexual penetration that happens without the consent of women, involves use of force, or threat of force, intimidation, and/or when the perpetrator attempts to incapacitate the victim by administrating alcohol/drug (Abeid et al., 2014). It is considered the sexual expression of control and anger (Groth & Birnbaum, 2013) within the context of women's subordinate position in society. Rape is deemed to be a 'global epidemic' affecting close to a billion of girls and women over their life (Equality Now, 2017). It is estimated that globally 14–25% of adult women have been raped and occurrence of child sexual abuse varies between 2% and 62% (Abeid et al., 2014). About 1 in 6 women and 1 in 33 men in America have been raped or have been the victim of an attempted rape in their lifetime and about 9 of every 10 rape victims are women and most of the perpetrators are men (Adams-Clark & Chrisler, 2018). As per the UN report, approximately 120 million girls throughout the world, close to 1 in 10, have been raped by the age of 20 (UNICEF, 2014). The UN Statistical Report (based on government registered rape cases of 65 selected countries) highlighted that more than 250,000 rape cases and attempted rape cases have been recorded annually by police (UNODC, 2005). Another report highlighted in the United Kingdom's daughter documentary – 2015 is that about 250 women in UK are raped daily and the rapists belong to every economic, social, and ethnic group (Singh, 2015). Despite its pervasiveness, most

DOI: 10.4324/9781032696058-4

sexual assaults and rapes are not filed to the police and when reported, prosecution and conviction are unlikely (Adams-Clark & Chrisler, 2018).

Present Study

As per the NCRB (2018) report, West Bengal is one of the top ten states in India in terms of reported incidences of rape (1,069 numbers cases). If the last six years NCRB reports are considered, it can be observed that since 2013–2018, not much variations have been observed regarding rape in West Bengal. Reported rape cases in Bengal somewhat varies from 1,685 in 2013 to 1,069 in 2018 even after strengthening the laws and massive awareness created after the outrage of '2012 Delhi Nirvaya case.' Yet, the available districts-level data (data.gov.in) shows that Bengal's reported rape cases have made an immense jump in the last decade. In 2002, the number of reported cases in Bengal was 758 which increased to 2,362 in 2011 and the growing trend still continues. Figure 4.1 shows the district-wise spatial intensity of incidences of rape (376 IPC) in Bengal during 2018 which reflects that the most vulnerable districts in West Bengal are North-24 Parganas, South-24 Parganas, Nadia, Murshidabad, Malda, Birbhum, Bardhaman, Purba and Paschim Medinipur, North Dinajpur, Cooch Behar, Jalpaiguri, and Darjeeling. The continuous occurrences of rape incidences in the past few years raise a big question about women safety in West Bengal. The brutal *Park Street (Kolkata) gang-rape* case in early 2012, the 2013 *Kamduni gang-rape and murder* case (Barasat, North-24 Parganas), *Madhyamgram gang-rape and suicidal* case (North-24 Parganas), the 2020 *Kumarganj gang-rape and murder* case (South Dinajpur) are incessantly the reminiscence of the brutality of middle era. In *Park Street (Kolkata) gang-rape* case, the victim was gang-raped by five men at gunpoint in a moving car on the night of February 6, 2012, and thrown out on Park Street in South Kolkata, which shocked the capital city (Kundu, 2016). In *Kamduni gang-rape and murder* case, a 20-year-old college girl in Kamduni village of Barasat, North-24 Parganas, was abducted and brutally gang-raped and murdered by nine men while returning home from college on June 7, 2013 (Bhabani, 2016). The culprits had tone apart her legs up to the naval and slit her throat before dumping her body in a pond. This dreadful 'Bengal's Nirvaya' incident sparked outrage across West Bengal. Another shocking incident happened in Madhyamgram, North-24 Parganas, on October 26, 2013, when a 16-year-old girl was allegedly gang-raped by seven men two times in two consecutive days. The most unfortunate incident happened when the girl set herself on fire (though her father alleged that the accused ablaze her daughter) on December 23, 2013, after tolerating continuous threat from the accused sides for withdrawing the police case (HT Correspondent, 2014). Not only South Bengal, women are not safe in North Bengal too (Staff Reporter, 2011). Recent *Kumarganj gang-rape and murder* case in South Dinajpur district of West Bengal is again reminiscence of the gruesome atrocities of 2019 Telengana

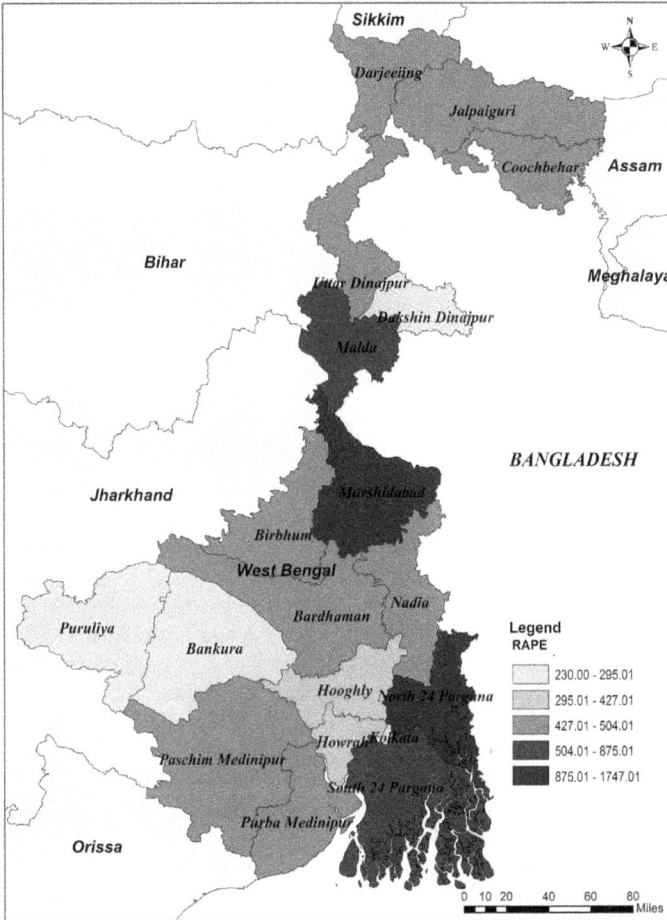

Figure 4.1 District-wise Spatial Intensity of Rape in West Bengal during 2018

Source: data.gov.in

gang-rape and murder case. In that case, a 17-year-old girl in Kumargaunj was gang-raped and murdered by three culprits (one is her boyfriend) and the culprits set ablaze her body near a culvert in pukurtala (Sen, 2020). In the past few years, incidence of child rape has been on the rise in West Bengal. In 2018, 2,240 POCSO cases (girl child victims only) have been registered in West Bengal which accounts for 5.77% of the national total (NCRB, 2018). Only in Kolkata, 227 POCSO cases have been registered (NCRB, 2018).

Since rape and sexual assaults are still considered taboo in West Bengal and it carries a serious social stigma, so far many cases have gone unreported. The rising incidences of rape again raise questions about girls and women safety in West Bengal. The fear of rape continuously restricts women movement in West Bengal. It is too often heard that society blames the victims for their misfortunes rather than rapists even in twenty-first century. So, the present study aims to understand the magnitude and spatiotemporal extent of rape in West Bengal, exhume the most noteworthy factors that endorse rape victimisation among women, and finally to suggest some situational environmental measures that might help the concerned authorities to undertake better initiatives to lessen the risk of rape victimisation among women in West Bengal.

Methodology

Sampling Techniques and Data Collection Tools

A comprehensive survey has been conducted to accumulate textured information about rape and sexual violence against women in West Bengal. Based on the preliminary information about most vulnerable districts in Bengal, the districts Kolkata, Murshidabad, Nadia, North-24 and South-24 Parganas, Malda, Birbhum, Bardhaman, and Jalpaiguri have been selected as sample sites for conducting intensive survey. To incorporate the utmost variation about perceptions within the respondents, stratified random sampling techniques have been used across different age, sex, economic, and social classes to select the sample population for conducting the survey. Therefore, in total 980 respondents from the sample districts belonging to different age, sex, educational standards, and professional backgrounds have been selected for in-depth fact-finding interviews based on pre-structured questionnaire schedule. In addition, 42 FGDs (a total of 250 participated members in the focus group) have been carried out with different stakeholders like police officials, BDOs (Block Development Officers) and SDOs (Sub-Divisional Officers), Gram Panchayat Pradhan(s) (chief of panchayat) and associates, several NGO members (who actively work to protect women's rights), advocates and teachers. Only those respondents were considered who agreeably participated in the interview and FGDs and shared their views and experiences. During the interview, the respondents were served by open-ended prompted questionnaires as individuals have their own views and understanding. Only to determine the factors responsible for increasing the risk of victimisation of rape among women, close-ended questionnaire was provided. Emphasis was on gathering information about demographics, rape acknowledgement, fear of rape, help-seeking and reporting, situational environment and rape, and so on. Direct interactions with respondents to explore people's perceptions at the societal levels make this method of data collection more convenient. Information obtained from

FGDs and questionnaire surveys have further been used to weighing up the attribute of rape and other forms of sexual annoyance in West Bengal.

Methods

In the present study, multiple methods have been adopted to reach the study objectives. Both qualitative and quantitative databases have been considered to conduct this study. The databases have been accumulating from various primary and secondary data sources. The fact-finding interviews were conducted with the willing respondents, FGDs with the stakeholders have been considered primary data sources. Whereas the NCRB reports, open government data (data.gov.in), FIRs (First Information reports), NGO records, and some well-circulated newspaper reports (*The Hindu, The Times of India, The Telegraph,* and *Anandabazar Patrika*) from 2016 to 2020 have been considered secondary data sources. After collecting both qualitative and quantitative data, these were tabulated and analysed using MS-Excel. The quantitative information collected from various secondary data sources and perceptions of the respondents gathered during fact-finding interviews and FGDs assist in portraying the magnitude and spatial extent of rape in West Bengal. Kernel density has been performed using ARC-GIS 10.1 software to determine the extent of rape hotspots in Murshidabad and Nadia districts based on police station–based FIRs on rape cases. Afterwards, to exhume the most noteworthy factors that exacerbate rape victimisation among women in West Bengal, factor analysis has been done. For this, a structured questionnaire consisting of 38 close-ended questions (say items or variables) under some possible factors (that have been derived from reviewing the existing literature, published government reports, newspaper reports, etc.) was prepared. The questionnaire consists of questions under aspects of societal stereotype beliefs and broader supportive attitudes, disorganised community and situational crime-prone environment, socio-economic adversity and supportive criminal activities, perpetrator's individual attitudes as well as relationship with delinquent peers and unsupportive family environment, legal aspects, and hostile physical environment and intensifying insecurities among women. These questions have been subjected to the FGD participants ($N = 250$) and were instructed to give weight with regard to all questions (or items) based on five-point Likert scale (Likert, 1932) ('strongly disagree' = '1' to 'strongly agree'= '5'). Afterwards, Cronbach's alpha reliability test (Cronbach, 1951) has been performed at all subscale dimensions to check internal consistency and reliability of the variables. Then KMO (Kaiser–Meyer–Olkin) and Bartlett's test of sphericity results are checked to test validity of the data. After securing sampling adequacy, exploratory factor analysis (EFA) is executed using extraction methods of principal component analysis to assess the underlying factor structures. (Note that EFA has been run to excavate underlying factor structure from a set of observed variables when minimum quantitative studies have been done regarding a measure) (Bandalos & Finney, 2010). Then 'factor loadings' (say coefficients) that relate variables to the extracted factors have been rotated (by performing varimax rotation) to ensure each factor has non-zero loadings and makes the factor matrix easy to interpret. Following rotation, the mean score has been calculated to determine the level of satisfaction among the FGD respondents about the factors of rape being obtained from EFA. The SPSS-20 version software has been used to perform the above statistics. Next, a micro-level assessment of anti-rape measures was conducted. Finally, some strategic situational crime prevention measures have been recommended so that the government could address this social issue more efficiently.

Critical Analysis

Information gathered from in-depth interviews, FGDs, and various secondary data sources help to make an in-depth understanding of the magnitude of incidences of rape, existing rape myths, and the most significant socio-economic and situational environmental backcloths of men's rape proclivity in West Bengal. The details have been discussed in the following sections.

Analysis of Secondary Data

Situation in Kolkata Metros

The analysis of the secondary information collected from various sources has provided a clear portrayal of the magnitude of abominable offence rape in West Bengal. The scenario of rape in Kolkata and suburbs has been portrayed from the information provided by criminal records section, Lalbazar, Kolkata. From this information, it can be illustrated that from 2010 to 2014, incidences of rape in Kolkata and surrounding suburb region have continuously increased, with 32 cases recorded in 2010 to 154 in 2014 (Table 4.1). If focus is given on Bengal's capital Kolkata, it can be noticed that, as per the very recently published NCRB (2018) report, only 15 rape cases have been reported to police. Even in 2016 and 2017, the numbers had remained 14 and 15, respectively (NCRB, 2016; NCRB, 2017). The trend analysis (Figure 4.2) of statistics provided by NCRB illustrates that from 2010 to 2013, the reported incidences of rape in the Kolkata metro have been following an increasing trend with 32 in 2010 to 75 in 2013. But after 2013, the numbers followed a gradually diminishing trend. The percentage change in 2018 over 2013 was about 80% (Table 4.2). It reflects a positive indication of government initiatives regarding women's safety in the Kolkata metropolitan, specifically after the notorious 'Delhi Nirvaya gang-rape and murder case' and 'Kolkata Park-Street gang rape case.' It is estimated that if the government

Table 4.1 Incidences of Rape (376 IPC) in Kolkata and Suburbs

Crime Heads	Year				
	2010	*2011*	*2012*	*2013*	*2014*
Rape	32	46	121	151	154

Source: Criminal Records Sections, Detective Department, Lalbar, Kolkata.

Table 4.2 Tabulation of Reported Cases of Rape (376 IPC) in Kolkata Metro (2010–2018)

Year	2010	2011	2012	2013	2014	2015	2016	2017	2018	% Change in 2018 over 2013
No. of victims	32	46	68	75	41	33	14	15	15	80.00

Percentage change in 2018 over 2013.

Source: NCRB report.

show such keenness in future, the incidences of rape in Kolkata metro will be less in coming years (Figure 4.2).

Spatial Distribution of Rape in Murshidabad District

By analysing the FIR reports provided by the Murshidabad district police, a microscale observation has been conducted. From the FIR reports, it can be observed that from December 2016 to December 2018, a total of 538 rape cases have been reported at different police stations (PS) in the Murshidabad district (Table 4.3). It again raises questions about women safety in this district. Figure 4.3 shows the spatial distributional pattern of hotspots of heinous crime rape in the Murshidabad district. It reflects that Berhampore, Domkal, Jalangi, Sagardighi, Farrakka, Suti II, Raghunathganj, Harihapara, and Murshidabad are the most vulnerable CD Blocks in this district. Under these vulnerable blocks, most cases have been reported from the areas under the police stations of Daulatabad, Jalangi, Sagardighi, Berhampore, Suti, Murshidabad, Farrakka, Harihapara, Islampur, and Jalangi (Table 4.3).

Spatial Distribution of Rape in Nadia District

Another micro-level observation has been made by analysing the two years FIR reports provided by Nadia District Police. The reports reveal that 90 cases were registered at different police stations in the Nadia district from

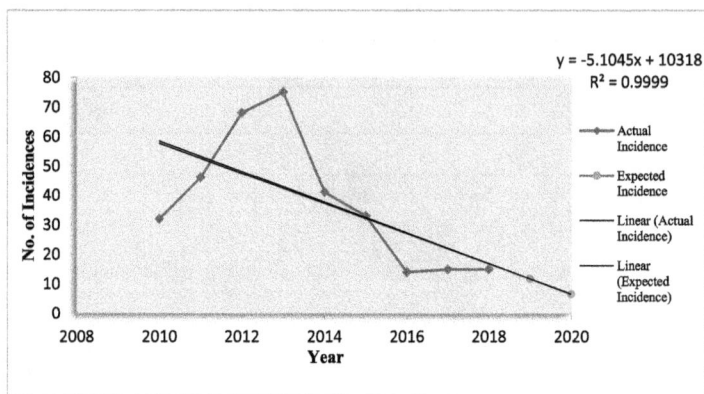

Figure 4.2 Trend Analysis of Incidences of Rape in Kolkata Metro (2010–2020)

Source: Author Computation

Table 4.3 Reported Rape Cases under the Murshidabad District Police (from December 2016 to December 2018)

Block Name	Name of the Police Station	No. of Cases	Block Name	Name of the Police Station	No. of Cases
	Barwan	17		Khargram	14
	Beldanga	12		Lalgola	16
	Berhampore	39		Murshidabad	23
	Berhampore Women Ps	7		Nabagram	10
	Bhagwangola	19		Nowda	9
	Bharatpur	11		Raghunathganj	13
	Daulatabad	10		Raninagar	17
	Domkal	74		Ranitala	11
	Farrakka	24		Rejinagar	10
	Harihapara	28		Sagardighi	32
	Islampur	25		Saktipur	3
	Jalangi	42		Salar	4
	Jangipur	6		Samsherganj	7
	Jiaganj	8		Suti	29
	Kandi	18		**Total**	538

Source: Murshidabad District Police Portal.

December 2016 to December 2018 (Table 4.4). From these FIR reports, the spatial extent of rape hotspots in this district developed in two years has been portrayed (Figure 4.4). This figure reflects that the most vulnerable CD Blocks in Nadia with regard to rape victimisation among women are Hanskhali, Chapra, Chakdaha, Ranaghat I and II, Nakashipara, and Tehatta

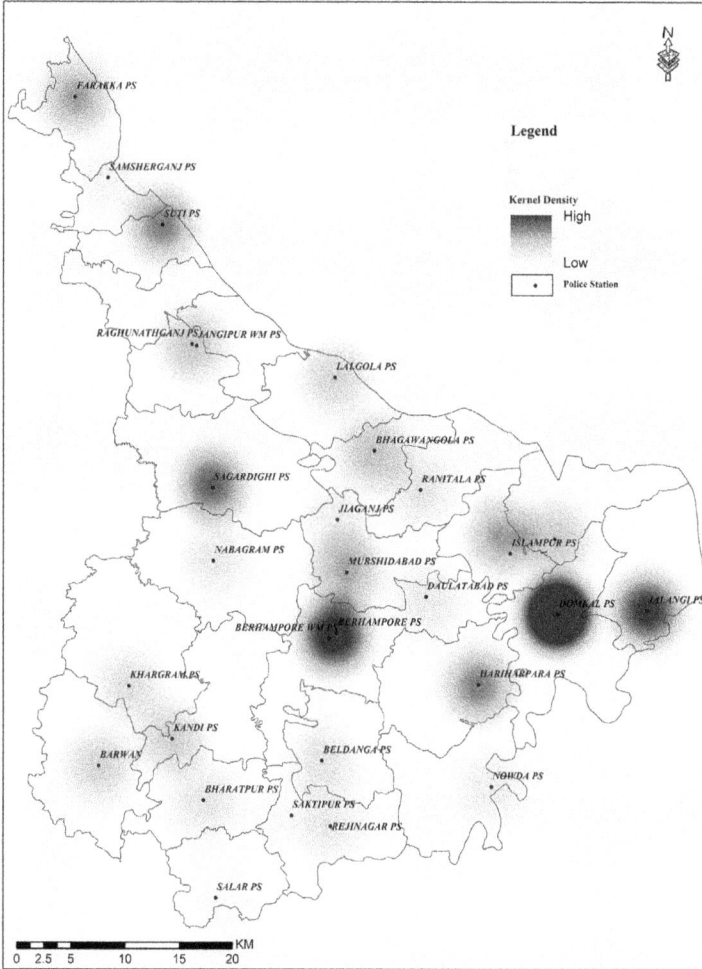

Figure 4.3 Spatial Extension of Incidences of Rape in the Murshidabad District

Source: Murshidabad District Police Portal (from December 2016 to December 2018)

I, although rape cases (Sec. 376 IPC) were registered more or less from all the CD Blocks. Among the vulnerable blocks, most cases were documented from the surrounding areas under police stations (PS) of Chapra, Hanskhali, Kalyani, Chakdaha, Tehatta, Nakashipara, and Kotyali (Table 4.4). Yet data on attempt to rape (Sec. 376/511 IPC) cases were not provided by this portal. But the previous NCRB reports reflect that those cases registered under Sec. 376/511 IPC were also very high in this district.

Fear of Rape

The respondents' opinions about this emerging issue are helpful in understanding women's susceptibility in West Bengal. A number of stereotype
notions regarding fear of rape, vulnerable groups, and non-reporting have
evolved from their opinions. Since this is a very burning social issue in recent
days, our surveyors did not face much difficulty in obtaining reliable information from the respondents, especially those living in urban areas. A complete picture of people's perceptions about rape in Bengal (derived from field

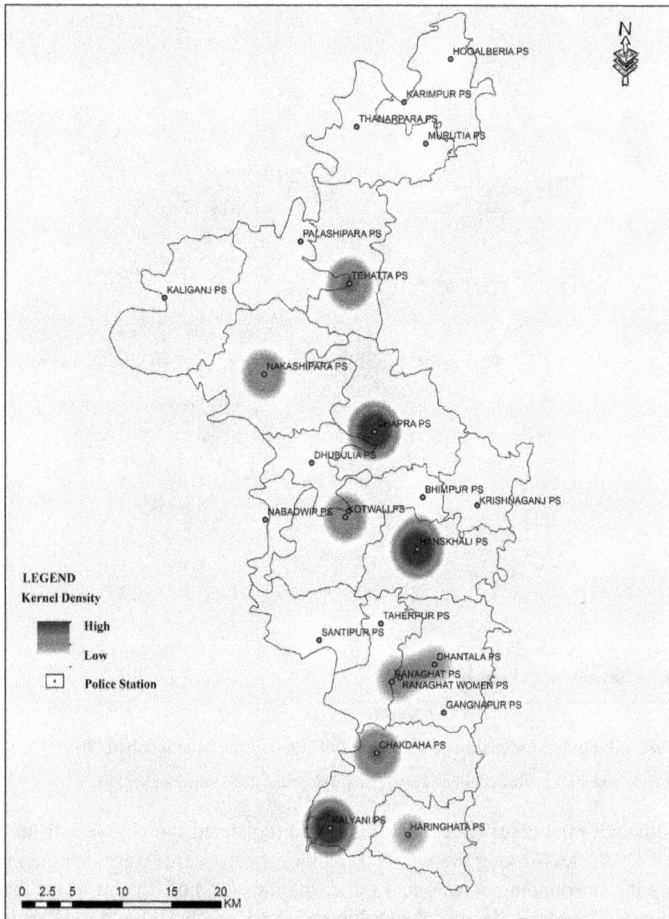

Figure 4.4 Spatial Extension of Incidences of Rape in the Nadia District
Source: Nadia District Police Portal (from December 2016 to December 2018)

Table 4.4 Reported Rape Cases under the Nadia District Police (from December 2016
to December 2018)

Block Name	Name of the Police Station	No. of Cases	Block Name	Name of the Police Station	No. of Cases
	Bhimpur	2		Krishnaganj	1
	Chakdaha	7		Krishnanagar Women	0
	Chapra	11		Murutia	2
	Dhantala	4		Nabadwip	1
	Dhubulia	1		Nakashipara	6
	Gangnapur	0		Palashipara	1
	Hanskhali	11		Ranaghat	2
	Haringhata	4		Ranaghat Women	3
	Hogalberia	2		Santipur	2
	Kaliganj	1		Taherpur	2
	Kalyani	11		Tehatta	7
	Karimpur	2		Thanarpara	1
	Kotyali	6	**Total**		**90**

Source: Nadia District Police Portal.

survey) has been portrayed in Table 4.5. From the opinion of the respondents,
it became clear that at present people (92.45% respondents) are very much
concerned about the safety of *Bengal's daughters* (Table 4.5). Fear of rape has
sprouted like wildfire among people in Bengal because of the events of rape
continuously published in the newspapers. It has been derived from the questionnaire survey that people from urban and semi-urban areas are comparatively more conscious about fear of rape compared to rural inhabitants. About
86.53% respondents (both male and female) confessed that they become worried when any female members of their family go outside from home, especially late evening. When stress has been given to access the proliferation
of risks only among the women respondents (N = 537), it is observed that
fear of being sexually harassed and raped has frightened the life of more or
less every respondent. Continuous feelings of insecurities and threats have
led to heavy supervision on their daily routine activities, restricted free movements, and enduring a myriad of frustrations on a day-to-day basis. About
76.35% of the respondents' concurred that while staying outside from home,
a relentless fright of being watched, hassling, sexual harassment, and rape
chase them. About 87.52% of women respondents replied that fear of rape
resulting in restrictions on moving out from home compel to avoid some areas
after sunset which seem to be comparatively safe during daytimes. So, they
try to complete their necessary outer work during the day. About 83.80% of
the respondents said that they try to abstain from going out alone, even their
parents never let them go. Again, 90.32% of respondents conveyed that they

avoid public transports (especially overnight bus, taxi services, long-distance overnight train journeys), crowded public places (e.g., crowded markets, parks, stations, bus stands, etc.), and secluded areas because the fear of being raped and sexually harassed chase them continuously. Fear of rape is obvious among the women respondents; about 91.25% (Table 4.5) of the respondents convey that they cannot trust anybody, even the close ones. They are in concordant with the fact that the number of stranger rapes is very less compared to incest rape and marital rape which are rarely disclosed. Even one-third of the married respondents also conveyed that most of the ever-married women have no clear conception about marital rape. They blindly believe in societal stereotype thinking that force intercourse is the right of their husbands. Moreover, attached social stigmas always inhibit them not to disclose their distress. Thus, the so-called husbands continuously showed their masculine supremacy and subordinate their wives. Therefore, most of the women respondents cannot rely upon their close relatives, friends, or anyone else blindly.

Determinants of Rape Victimisation in West Bengal

In this present study, the results of factor analysis are very much effective in excavating the most significant factors that exacerbate the risk among women of being victims of rape and sexual harassment in West Bengal. With due course 17 responses have been marked as less reliable as high level of inconsistency has been noticed among their opinions as per value considered in Likert scale and they answered less than 15% of the questions; this did not meet the threshold percentage outlined by Johnson (2003) for expulsion. Therefore, acceptable numbers of responses were 233 with a response rate of 93.20%. A wide range of recommendations regarding minimum sample size (N) in factor analysis exist. Guilford (1954) recommended that minimum sample size (N) should be at least 200; Cattell (1978) suggested ideal number of N should be minimum 250. Moreover, MacCallum et al. (1999) suggested for consideration of the level of communality of the variables to determine the minimum sample size population in factor analysis. According to them, the desirable mean level of communality of the variables should be at least 0.7. Therefore, the sample size population ($N = 233$) in this study is seem to be appropriate as mean level communalities, $M = 0.920$ and the range of communalities of all the 38 determinant variables varies from 0.657 to 0.987 (Appendix 7). The resulting Cronbach's alpha coefficient value for each level is more than 0.7 (standard value advocated by Cronbach (1951) and accepted in most of the social science research work) (Bland & Altman 1997; Nunnally, 1978) which ensure strong internal consistency within the variables (Appendix 7). The overall alpha coefficient value is 0.986, which also indicates strong internal consistency and reliability in-between the variables (Appendix 7). Regarding validity of the sample, the resulting KMO value of 0.804 indicates the distribution is adequate for conducting factor analysis. Moreover,

Table 4.5 Perceptions of the Respondents

		Frequency (F)			Percentage (%)
Acknowledgement of rape					
Concerned about the rising incidences of street harassment, eve-teasing, hassling, rape, incest rape, marital rape in society	N = 980	906	Male Female	369 537	40.73 59.27
Have no idea of rape and sexual harassment		74	Male Female	41 33	55.41 44.59
Measures of fear of rape (considered only acknowledged respondents, N = 906)					
Getting worried when a female member goes outside from home	N = 906 (considered both male and female respondents)	784			86.53
Continuous fear of being watched, bullied, hassling, sexual harassment, eve-teasing, rape while staying outside from home	N = 537 (considered female respondents only)	410			76.35
Try to complete all the necessary outer work before evening		470			87.52
Avoid going out alone, even parents do not allow to go outside alone		450			83.80
Try to avoid public transport, public places, secluded areas specifically after evening		485			90.32
Cannot trust anybody, even close ones		490			91.25

Source: Field survey.

the Bartlett's test of sphericity results (taking 95% confidence level, $\alpha = 0.05$) with *p*-value (sig.) of 0.000 is <0.05 and the approximate chi-square (χ^2) value is 26878.147 with a high degree of freedom (df) strongly rejecting the null hypothesis (H_0) (i.e., $r = 0$) and accepting the alternative hypothesis (H_1), that is, significant correlation exists in-between the variables. A significance value of Bartlett's test of sphericity <0.05 also specifies that the data do not produce an identity matrix (factor analysis would be worthless with an identity matrix) and are thus appropriately multivariate normal and suitable for factor analysis (George & Mallery, 2003). Hence, significance value of 0.000 in this analysis clearly indicates that factor analysis seems to be the appropriate method for further analysis of the datasets. In this study, exploratory factor analysis (EFA) has been performed for clubbing the variables into most suitable factors as EFA is used to find out underlying dimensionality of a set of variables (Field, 2000). From the factor loadings (Appendix 7) of the observed variables (items/questions) after varimax rotation with Kaiser normalisation resulting from EFA, it has been revealed that 38 variables (items/ questions) have been clubbed into 5 major factors having eigenvalue greater than 1. These factors have been named as follows: societal foster beliefs and attitudes; individual perpetrator's attitude and socio-economic adversity; relationship factors; legal and deterrence factors; and adverse physical environmental factors, respectively, after taking into consideration the relative intimacy of the correlated variables (having considered significant factor loadings of 0.50 and above) (Pal & Bagai, 1987) under each factor. These five factors collectively explained 92.02% of the total variance.

Table 4.6 represents the mean scores that help recognise the satisfaction level among the respondents regarding the extracted factors of rape and sexual abuse in Bengal. From this table, it can be stated that the initial factors, that is, societal foster beliefs and attitudes and individual perpetrator's attitude and socio-economic adversity, have explained maximum variables (13.28% and 10.82%, respectively, after rotation) but majority of them agreed that adverse physical environment, relationship factors, individual perpetrator's attitude, and socio-economic adversity factors are mostly liable for occurrence of incidences of rape and sexual assaults in West Bengal.

Evaluation of Anti-rape Measures and Strategic Recommendations

Rape and other forms of sexual violence against women affect not only a women's life but also the entire society in general. So, diminishing such nuisance and developing a rape-free society, India has undertaken several regulatory measures. The nationwide outcry after the brutal incidence of '2012 Delhi Nirvaya gang-rape and murder case' led to introduce the Criminal Law

Table 4.6 Mean Score

Significant Factors of Rape	N	Minimum	Maximum	Mean	Std. Deviation
Societal foster beliefs and attitudes	233	1.00	5.00	3.89	0.86
Individual perpetrator's attitude and socio-economic adversity	233	1.00	5.00	**4.01**	0.90
Relationship factors	233	1.33	5.00	**4.09**	0.75
Legal and deterrence factors	233	1.00	5.00	3.96	0.98
Adverse physical environment	233	1.00	5.00	**4.13**	0.86
Valid *N* (listwise)	233				

Source: Computed by author.

(Amendment) Act in 2013 which broadened the definition of rape and toughen the punishment procedures. Moreover, the Criminal Law (Amendment) Act, 2018, has been introduced by the parliament after the nationwide protests of the renowned Kathua gang-rape and murder of a minor girl in January 2018 in the then Jammu and Kashmir. This Act put the death penalty as a possible punishment for raping a girl below 12 years. Besides, the Government of India has already set up statutory bodies such as National Commission for Women, Ministry of Women and Child Development to protect the women's rights in India, provide a voice for their issues and concerns, advise the government about policies, schemes, and programmes regarding women rights, and so on. The government also put effort to set up fast-track courts. Innovative awareness campaigns like *Beti Padhao, Beti Bachao* have been undertaken. The West Bengal state government has also undertaken many initiatives to ensuring women's basic rights and lessen susceptibilities of rape and other forms of sexual violence. For that the Ministry of Women and Children Development and Social Welfare has been established by the state government for policy formulation and supervision and to ensure basic rights of women and minors. The *West Bengal Commission for Women* is another statutory body that is also established for mitigating all forms of women issues in Bengal. The Bengal government also stressed on setting up more women police stations across all the districts. Emphasis given on continual capacity-building of the state by introducing more CCTV surveillance, stringent patrolling, and vigilance, specifically after dark in the hotspot regions, provides advantages of online FIR registration portal; Women Grievance Cells develop separate body of *Department of Child Development* to ensure child rights and security, provide free medical care (included private hospitals also) and legal aids to the raped victims, and launch toll-free helpline numbers. West Bengal government also stressed upon making women self-reliant. So, many schools, colleges, and even the law enforcement departments themselves take initiatives to arrange self-defence training programme for the young girls and women to make them self-reliant. Despite such potential initiatives undertaken by both the central and state governments, such inhuman nuisance against women in Bengal is yet to be exterminated. Although stringent laws are a great step in dealing with this problem, these are not enough. As observed, stricter laws in the aftermath of the 2012 Delhi Nirvaya gang-rape and murder case have led to higher levels of reporting in Bengal as well as in whole India but did not necessarily improve the conviction rates and faster investigations procedures. Still, West Bengal has witnessed many such inhuman practice of rape and ablaze death in recent days. Therefore, questions arise: Are the strengthen laws not enough to fabricate dread among the accused? Are all the government policies limited to only strengthening laws and ensuring women security? Are there any initiatives taken to annihilate stereotype societal beliefs, improve individual perpetrators' attitudes, and undertake policies related to betterment of the immediate situational environment (physical and social environment)?

If already taken, is there any gap between policy formation and implementations? Hence, strategies should be more efficient and precise. This study tried to suggest some additional measures in tandem with the government initiatives that might help the government to improve capacity-building to provide more safety and lessen the opportunities to commit rape and thus minimise sexual victimisation among women in Bengal:

1. The government need to take measures like introducing more formal and informal guardians, such as emphasising 24*7 hours police patrolling, introducing more streetlights, CCTV cameras in every risk-prone areas like crowd-less roads, lanes, school, college and university premises, parks, cinema halls, bus terminus, railway stations, industrial belt areas, brick line fields, and other public areas and abundant places irrespective of villages and cities; improve community connectivity; and promote neighbourhood watch. Special focus needs to be given on the most vulnerable districts in Bengal, namely Nadia, Murshidabad, North-24 and South-24 Parganas, North and South Dinajpur, Jalpaiguri, Bardhaman, Birbhum, and so on.

2. District police need to give preference on mapping the potential risk-prone areas under different police stations using the help of GIS (Geographic Information System) and upload all information on their web portal. The potential risk-map might be helpful for the law enforcement officials to tighten formal and informal security in those areas, thus reducing crime opportunities to the rapists and minimising rape victimisation among women.

3. The central government on September 20, 2018, has launched National Database on Sexual Offenders (NDSO) that contains details of the accused convicted under charges of rape, gang-rape, POCSO, molestation, and sexual harassment. Such portal needs to be developed at the state level.

4. The Bengal government need to stress on signing more MOU (memorandum of understanding) with public–private–partnership (PPP) to ensure more safety of women in public space. With this collaboration, the government may give up the security responsibilities of several government offices, schools, colleges, universities, public libraries, and so on, to private security companies to ensure women's safety.

5. On July 2018, the Kolkata police have introduced a special all-women patrolling team 'The Winners' to combat and prevent crimes such as eve-teasing, molestation, and so on to make the city safer for women. The well-trained all-women motorbike squads cover the entire jurisdiction of the Kolkata police; they keep bird's-eye views on schools, colleges, parks, cinema halls; and they can reach even the remote areas of the city at any time. More such effective initiatives needed to be introduced under all the districts police in West Bengal.

6. Nowadays, the West Bengal government in association with some NGOs has already taken many school–college-based initiatives like training of

Karate and martial arts to make the girls and women self-reliant. Like the Bidhannagar Police Commissionerate in September 2018 organised a self-defence programme at the salt-lake stadium named *Sukonnya* to make women self-dependent. However, most of these moves are limited to metropolitan cities only. It is needed to be introduced in remote rural areas also.

7. The government need to ensure the security of women in public transports. So, priority should be given to increase proper vigilance in public transports especially at night. There must be protocols to set up CCTV cameras in every public transport; the cab drivers, bus drivers, and conductors must disclose their identity card during service time, and so on. The RPF (Railway Protection Force) should give strict instructions to strengthen night patrolling to ensure women's safety in long-distance train journeys.

8. These days the incidences of ablaze death after raping the victim(s) are increasing. The accused seem that it is one of the easiest paths to hide their crime. So, the government needs to take immediate action to check the proper execution of 'The Poison Possession and Sale Rules, 2013' (Writ Petition order date July 18, 2013) in order to limit the counter-sell of petrol, diesel, and kerosene in the open markets.

Moreover, focus should be on enriching morality through formal education and social interactions, poverty alleviation and employment generation, community-based awareness programmes arranged by the local government at the municipality and panchayat levels aiming to change the foster beliefs and attitudes of general people in society, reduction in gender gap, increase in legal awareness, and minimising victimisation of rape among women.

References

Abeid, M., Muganyizi, P., Olsson, P., Darj, E., & Axemo, P. (2014). Community perceptions of rape and child sexual abuse: A qualitative study in rural Tanzania. *BMC International Health and Human Rights*, *14*(1), 23.

Adams-Clark, A. A., & Chrisler, J. C. (2018). What constitutes rape? The effect of marital status and type of sexual act on perceptions of rape scenarios. *Violence Against Women*, *24*(16), 1867–1886.

Bandalos, D. L., & Finney, S. J. (2010). Exploratory and confirmatory factor analysis. In *Quantitative methods in the social and behavioral sciences: A guide for researchers and reviewers*. Routledge.

Bhabani, S. (2016, January 29). West Bengal: Kamduni victim's kin want death for rapists. *India Today*. Retrieved February 7, 2020, from www.indiatoday.in/mail-today/story/west-bengal-kamduni-victims-kin-want-death-for-rapists-306043-2016-01-29

Bland, J. M., & Altman, D. G. (1997). Statistics notes: Cronbach's alpha. *BMJ, 314*(7080), 572.

Cattell, R. B. (1978). *The scientific use of factor analysis in behavior and life sciences.* Plenum.

Cronbach, L. J. (1951). Coefficient alpha and the internal structure of tests. *Psychometrika, 16*(3), 297–334. https://doi.org/10.1007/bf02310555.

Equality Now. (2017, November 7). *The world's shame: The global rape epidemic.* Retrieved February 16, 2020, from www.equalitynow.org/resource/the-worlds-shame-the-global-rape-epidemic/

Field, A. (2000). *Discovering statistics using SPSS for windows.* SAGE Publications.

George, D., & Mallery, P. (2003). *SPSS for windows step by step: A simple guide and reference. 11.0 update* (p. 549). wps.ablongman.com/wps/media/objects/385.George4answerspdf

Groth, A. N., & Birnbaum, H. J. (2013). *Men who rape: The psychology of the offender.* Springer.

Guilford, J. P. (1954). *Psychometric methods* (2nd ed.). McGraw-Hill.

HT Correspondent. (2014, January 1). Kolkata erupts in protest over Madhyamgram rape victim's death. *Hindustan Times.* Retrieved February 7, 2020, from www.hindustantimes.com/india/kolkata-erupts-in-protest-over-madhyamgram-rape-victim-s-death/story-WOJbQIDvdak3X2S5xnVLtK.html

Johnson, M. L. (2003). *Lose something? Ways to find your missing data* (Series 17-09). Houston Center for Quality of Care and Utilization Studies Professional Development. In Presti, R. L., Barca, E., & Passarella, G. (2010). A methodology for treating missing data applied to daily rainfall data in the Candelaro River Basin (Italy). *Environmental Monitoring and Assessment, 160*(1–4), 1.

Kundu, I. (2016, September 30). Kolkata Park Street rape case: Main accused Kader Khan arrested from Delhi. *India Today.* Retrieved February 7, 2020, from www.indiatoday.in/india/story/kolkata-park-street-rape-case-main-accused-arrested-delhi-344060-2016–09–30

Likert, R. (1932). A technique for the measurement of attitudes. *Archives of Psychology, 22*(140), 1–55.

MacCallum, R. C., Widaman, K. F., Zhang, S., & Hong, S. (1999). Sample size in factor analysis. *Psychological Methods, 4*(1), 84.

NCRB. (2016). *Crime in India: Statistics-2018*, National Crime Records Bureau, Ministry of Home Affairs, Government of India, New Delhi. https://ncrb.gov.in/

NCRB. (2017). *Crime in India: Statistics-2018*, National Crime Records Bureau, Ministry of Home Affairs, Government of India, New Delhi. https://ncrb.gov.in/

NCRB. (2018). *Crime in India: Statistics-2018.* National Crime Records Bureau, Ministry of Home Affairs, Government of India. https://ncrb.gov.in/en

Nunnally, J. C. (1978). *Psychometric testing.* McGraw Hill.

Pal, Y., & Bagai, O. P. (1987). *A common factory better reliability approach to determine the number of interpretable factors.* IX Annual Conference of the Indian Society for Probability and Statistics Held at Delhi, University of Delhi, India.

Sen, K. (2020, January 8). Teen raped, killed and brunt. *The Telegraph.* Retrieved February 9, 2020, from www.telegraphindia.com/states/ west-bengal/teen-raped-killed-and-burnt/cid/1733886

Singh, H. (2015, March 12). United Kingdom's daughters, an Indian man's response to BBC's documentary on Delhi gang rape. *The Indian Express.* Retrieved January 18, 2020, from https://indianexpress.com/article/india/ india-others/united-kingdoms-daughters-an-indian-mans-response-to-bbcs-documentary-on-delhi-gangrape/

Staff Reporter. (2011, February 16). Girl chasers stab boy to death, DM's guards 100m away refuse to step. *The Telegraph.* Retrieved February 9, 2020, from www.telegraphindia.com/india/girl-chasers-stab-boy-to-death-dm-s-guards-100m-away-refuse-to-step-in/cid/427391

UNICEF. (2014). *Hidden in plain sight: A statistical analysis of violence against children.* Data and Analytics Section Division of Data, Research and Policy. Cited in Rawat, R., & Masthanaiah, T. (2015). Explosion of rape cases in India: A study of last one decade. *International Journal of Current Research, 7*(7), 17976–17984.

UNODC (2005). *The Eighth United Nations survey on crime trends and the operations of criminal justice systems (2001–2002).* United Nations Office on Drugs and Crime. Retrieved January 18, 2020, from www.unodc.org/ unodc/en/data-and-analysis/Eighth-United-Nations-Survey-on-Crime-Trends-and-the-Operations-of-Criminal-Justice-Systems.html. Cited in Rawat, R., & Masthanaiah, T. (2015). Explosion of rape cases in India: A study of last one decade. *International Journal of Current Research, 7*(7), 17976–17984.

Bibliography

National Crime Record Bureau (NCRB). Ministry of Home Affairs, Govt. of India. http://ncrb.gov.in/

Open Government Data, Government of India. https://data.gov.in/

5 Domestic Violence against Women in West Bengal

Understanding Socio-psychological Milieu

Background and Context

The most common form of atrocity that women face throughout the world is 'domestic violence,' representing the violation of women's basic rights and a major public health issue (Garcia-Moreno et al., 2006; Haque et al., 2022). In broad sense, domestic violence includes all physical, sexual, psychological, or financial acts of violence or threats and abuses that might be committed in a domestic environment by a family member or an intimate partner. The World Health Organisation (WHO) defines domestic violence as a 'range of sexually, psychologically, and physically coercive acts used against women by current or former male intimate partners,' implying that domestic violence encompasses more than physical violence (WHO, 1997). Internationally, one in every three women is beaten, coerced into sex, or abused in their life by a member of her own family (WHO, 2013). A recent study conducted by WHO (2017) reveals that globally the domestic violence victimisation of women is around 30%, with considerably higher prevalence in South-East Asia (Peltzer & Pengpid, 2014; Doku & Asante, 2015). In almost 50 countries around the world, 10–52% of women reported physical or other forms of atrocity by their intimate partner at some point in their life (Heise et al., 1999; Krantz & Garcia-Moreno, 2005). A multi-country study conducted by WHO estimates that the lifetime pervasiveness of physical violence experienced by ever-partnered women falls between 4% and 49% and lifetime pervasiveness of sexual violence by intimate partner lies between 6% and 59%, with most sites between 10% and 50% (Kelmendi, 2015). Nowadays, the prevalence of domestic violence in intimate relationships is a major concern in developed countries. A study conducted by Miller (2006) shows that in the United States, about 19% of women were victims of physical violence at the hands of their intimate male partners. Furthermore, the WHO estimates that in developed countries, the lifetime prevalence of partner violence ranges from 13% in Japan to 61% in Peru, with most of the surveyed countries falling between 23% and 49% (Garcia-Moreno et al., 2006). Researchers have estimated that about 25% of women face domestic violence at some point in their lives

DOI: 10.4324/9781032696058-5

and more than 40% sustain physical grievance from these assaults (Tjaden & Thoennes, 2000). Hence, domestic violence victimisation is increasingly being recognised as causing noteworthy adverse health consequences among women (Stephenson et al., 2013). Such form of violence considerably affects women's mental, physical, sexual, and reproductive health (Garcia-Moreno & Stöckl, 2009; Chandra et al., 2009). Extensive forms of domestic violence by intimate partners sometimes have significant noxious effects on women's sexual and reproductive health like unwanted pregnancy (Khan et al., 1996), genital injuries, gynaecological disorders (Golding and Taylor, 1996), and large-scale mental health impacts (UNICEF, 2000). According to Sarkar (2008), preterm delivery, neonatal death, and low birthweight are the most excruciating agony women face as adverse outcomes of domestic violence victimisation during pregnancy. Furthermore, depressive symptoms, anxiety, suicidal attempts, and post-traumatic stress disorders are the most common forms of mental health outcomes reported among women who face domestic violence in their life (Falsetti, 2007; Chandra et al., 2009).

Present Study

Over the past few decades, the state of West Bengal in India has been facing a high prevalence of domestic violence victimisation among women. Almost every woman in West Bengal irrespective of all socio-economic status and cultural subgroups has faced domestic violence in their life. As per the national records released in 2018, West Bengal holds the top position in India, with 16,951 cases reported under Sec. 498-A IPC of domestic violence against women (NCRB, 2018). Taking into account the recent trends of domestic violence against women during 2013–2018, it can be said that during these six years, reported incidences (as per the NCRB report) in Bengal did not vary much. In 2013, the total cases registered under Sec. 498-A IPC in Bengal was 18,116, eventually followed by a parallel rising trend in the next three consecutive years (i.e., 23,278, 20,163, and 19,302 cases, respectively). Afterwards, the numbers gradually decreased with 16,800 and 16,951 cases registered in 2017 and 2018, respectively (Figure 5.1). Likewise, a total of 481 dowry death cases were reported in 2013, followed by a rising trend over the last six years (Figure 5.1). The rate of domestic violence also ranges from 40.78% in 2013 to 35.9% in 2018 reported under Sec. 498-A IPC and from 1.08% to 0.9% for dowry death cases.

Yet, the district-level data[1] also reflects that the incidences of domestic violence victimisation among women in West Bengal have increased dramatically over the past decade. In 2002, the district-wise total number of reported cases under Sec. 498-A and Sec. 304-B IPC in West Bengal were 3,859 and 265, respectively, followed by an immense jump in 2008 (with 13,663 and 451, respectively) and have continued to increase since then (Figure 5.2). Figures 5.3 and 5.4 respectively illustrate the spatial intensity of dowry deaths (Sec. 304-B

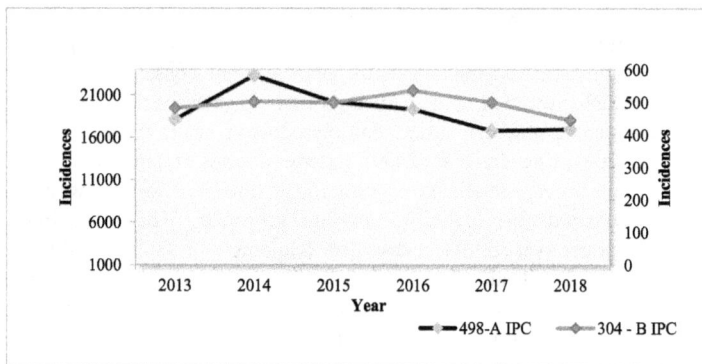

Figure 5.1 Reported Incidences of Domestic Violence against Women in West Bengal (2013–2018)

Source: NCRB Report

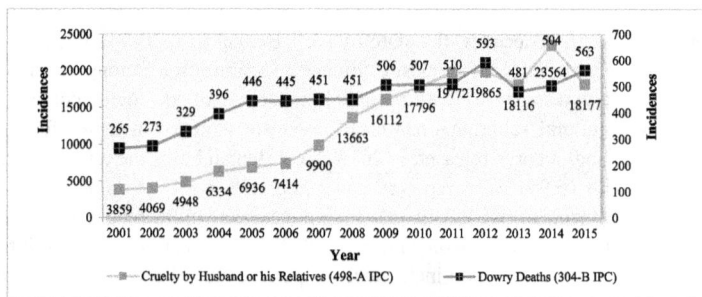

Figure 5.2 Trends of Domestic Violence against Women in West Bengal during 2002–2015

Source: data.gov.in

IPC) and cruelty by husband and his relatives (Sec. 498-A IPC) in West Bengal, based on 2018 district-level data.[2] From these, it is observed that in 2018, the districts most vulnerable to dowry death cases were Howrah, North-24 Parganas, Murshidabad, Nadia, Hooghly, Paschim Medinipur, Jalpaiguri, and South-24 Parganas. Cases under 498-A IPC were foremost in North-24 and South-24 Parganas, Howrah, Murshidabad, Nadia, and Hooghly districts. This obviously envisages how women in West Bengal face domestic violence in their everyday lives and raises questions about women's safety even within the so-called safest environment, their own homes and very often by the person whom they blindly trust. The patriarchal society in West Bengal socialises women in such

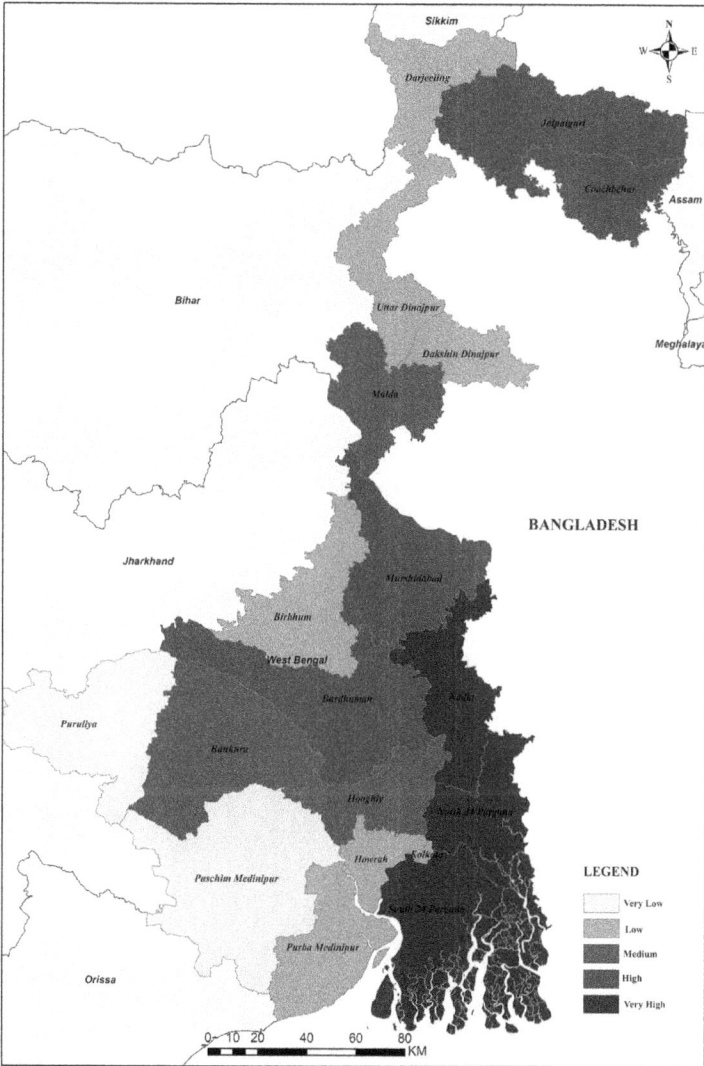

Figure 5.3 District-wise Intensity of Dowry Death Cases (under Sec. 304-B IPC) in West Bengal during 2018

Source: data.gov.in

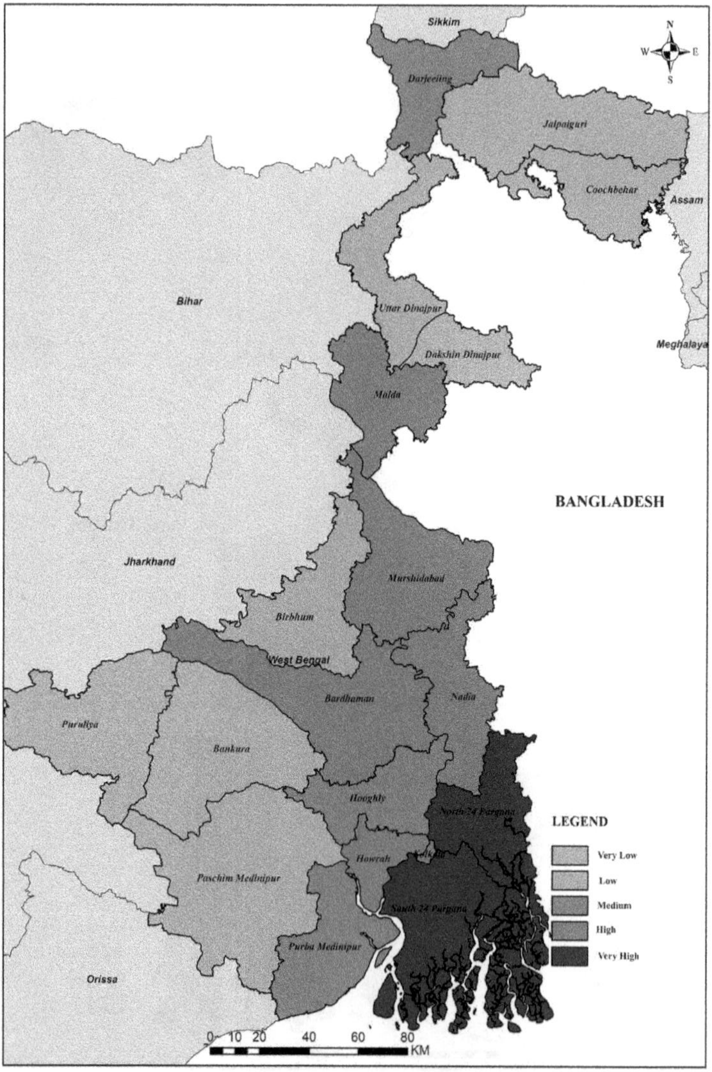

Figure 5.4 District-wise Intensity of Cruelty Cases (under Sec. 498-A IPC) by Husband and His Relatives in West Bengal during 2018

Source: data.gov.in

a way that despite facing extreme physical and psychological health concerns, they accept domestic violence, rationalise it, and rarely cry for help. Even in the twenty-first century, it is often heard in West Bengal that many married women commit suicide or are killed for inability to meet the high demand for dowry from their parental home. The present study thus aims to understand the magnitude of domestic violence against women in West Bengal, underneath the noteworthy determinants that endorse domestic violence victimisation, and suggest some situational environmental measures to curb this social issue.

Methodology

Sampling Techniques and Data Collection Tools

A comprehensive cross-sectional survey has been conducted to aggregate an in-depth understanding of the prevalence of domestic violence experienced by ever-married women in West Bengal. Based on the prevailing secondary information concerning the most domestic violence-prone districts in Bengal, the districts of Kolkata, Hooghly, Howrah, Murshidabad, Malda, Nadia, Birbhum, North-24 and South-24 Parganas, Paschim Medinipur, and Jalpaiguri have been selected as sample districts for conducting the intensive survey. Only 15–49 years of reproductive age groups of women have been considered for accomplishing this survey. To determine the absolute variations in perceptions of domestic violence among the respondents, stratified random sampling techniques have solely been adopted across varying ages, educational standards, and socio-economic settings (Teddlie, 2007). So, a total of 1,240 ever-married women of varying reproductive ages, communities, occupations, and educational qualifications from the sample districts have been selected as the sample population for in-detailed fact-finding interviews based on a prearranged questionnaire schedule. Besides, in total 27 focus group discussions (FGDs) have been conducted with different stakeholders who are vigorously working to protect women's rights, namely, police officials, advocates, SDOs (Sub-Divisional Officers), BDOs (Block Development Officers), Gram Panchayat Pradhan(s) (chief of panchayat) and associates, and several members of NGOs to make a vivid understanding of women's forbearance attitude and justification of domestic violence in society. Only those respondents who voluntarily consented to the interview were considered for the in-depth interviews and FGDs. During the interview, open-ended prompted questionnaires were served to the respondents as individuals have their own notions and views. Emphasis has been given to accumulating information regarding demographics, experiences of domestic violence over the last 12 months, frequencies and acuteness, acceptance attitudes by women themselves and society, help-seeking behaviour, socio-ecological environment pertaining to domestic violence against women, and so on. In addition to formal interviews and FGDs, some informal natural discussions have been conducted with the respondents regarding age-long inhumane social practices. Data acquired from the direct field surveys have been used to measure the genre of domestic violence against women in West Bengal.

Variables of Interest

Variables included in this study are dependent variables, that is, experience of domestic violence by ever-married women, and some likely independent variables derived from existing literature, fact-finding interviews, and FGDs. Here the dependent variable 'domestic violence' is defined as if a woman is physically, sexually (forced sex and substance use, e.g., alcohol, drugs), or verbally mistreated by her husband or his relatives, or the husband often threatens to divorce her or marry another woman at any point of time after marriage. The selected independent variables or say factors persuading domestic violence were the victim's age, educational qualification, age at marriage, the community of origin, working status, confronting behaviour, acceptance attitude, awareness of legal aids, child sex, household head sex, and household economic condition.

Two composite indices, namely 'women's acceptance attitude regarding domestic violence is justified' and 'confronting behaviour,' are the significant determinants of domestic violence victimisation among women in West Bengal. The variables that have been considered to make composite indices of women's acceptance attitude include the following: If a wife does not obey her husband, do you think he is justified in yelling at her? If a wife does not obey her husband, do you think he is justified in hitting, kicking, or beating her? Do you think that a woman has no right to deny sex with her husband even if she does not want to? Do you think that wife beating is justified if the husband suspects his wife is unfaithful? Do you think that a wife beating is justified if the wife goes out without telling her husband? Do you think that wife beating is justified if the wife neglects the house or children? Do you think that wife beating is justified if the wife shows disrespect for in-laws? Do you think that wife beating is justified if the natal family does not give money or other items as dowry? The respondents were asked to assign weight with respect to all variables (or questions or items) based on five-point Likert scale (Likert, 1932) ranging from '1' (strongly agree) to '5' (strongly disagree). After that, the responses were summed up concerning each respondent to get the total value of the index.

Similarly, the 'women's confronting behavioural index' has been conducted considering the variables included- Do you think women do not have to report domestic violence to law enforcement officials or share it with family members or friends? Do you think a general fear of police restrain women from reporting domestic violence? Do you think women are afraid to report domestic violence thinking about themselves or their child's future? Does attached social stigmas of losing family reputation constrain women from reporting domestic violence? The responses were given scores based on a five-point Likert scale ('1'= 'strongly agree' to '5'= 'strongly disagree') and afterwards they were summed up to get the total index value. After getting the composite index, the women's acceptance attitude score is divided into three groups, that is, *agree, sometimes agree*, and *disagree* and the confronting behavioural score is grouped into three, that is, *never confront, sometimes confront*, and *always confront* by using the formula: (maximum–minimum)/3.

Socio-demographic Characteristics of the Respondents

The average age of the studied women was 28.94 years (Standard Deviation, SD = 10.52). Most of the respondents were of urban origin (57.8%). Educational qualifications comprise 'no or primary level' (17%), 'secondary or higher secondary level' (46.3%), and 'graduation and above' (36.7%). About 59.8% of respondents were married at the age of 25 and above. The Working status of women comprised 'salaried jobs' (40.7%), 'housewife' (38.0%) and 'self-employed' (21.3%). About 38.4% of the participants belonged to the higher economic class, 36.9% were from the medium economic class, and 24.7% were from the lower economic class. The number of respondents not having children was 17.9%. Nearly 28.7% of respondents have son child only. About 17.7% of them have daughters only and the remaining 35.6% of respondents have sons and daughters both. Women's exposure to the outer world and mass media comprised 'yes' (18.5%), 'sometimes' (35.4%), and 'no' (46.1%). Household head sex included 'male' (41.4%) and 'female' (58.6%). Respondent's acceptance attitude towards domestic violence or agreeing with wife beating is justified at any reason ranges from 'disagree' (59.6%), 'sometimes' (14.1%), and 'agree' (26.3%). Being aware of existing legal aids pertaining to domestic violence included 'yes' (54.3%), 'somewhat' (26.7%), and 'no' (19.0%). Nearly 29.6% of respondents conveyed that they never confront domestic violence and around 24.4% and 45.9% of them confront sometimes and always, respectively.

Methods

In the present study, integrated methods have been applied to meet the study objectives. The fact-finding direct field interviews with the willing respondents and FGDs with the stakeholders have been considered primary data sources. However, the NCRB reports, district-level open government data (data.gov.in), FIRs, and NGO records have been deemed as secondary data sources. Once the databases were generated, these were then tabulated and analysed using MS-Excel. The quantitative data accumulated from secondary data sources and the notions and intent of the respondents assembled through the fact-finding interviews and FGDs help in delineating the magnitude of domestic violence against women in West Bengal. While constructing the composite scores of 'women's acceptance attitude' and 'confronting behaviour,' Cronbach's alpha reliability test (Cronbach, 1951) was performed to assess the internal consistency among the variables. Bivariate analysis has been done to examine the association in-between each dependent and independent variables. In the first bivariate analysis, a chi-square test was performed to evaluate the association between types of domestic violence experiences among the respondents and the perpetrators engaged in such abhorrent behaviour. Another chi-square test under the bivariate analysis has also been conducted to measure the differentials of domestic violence among the ever-married women over the past 12 months by background characteristics. Afterwards, multivariate analysis in the form of binary logistic regression has been performed to understand the strength of the association of the determinants that enhance the likelihood of victimisation of domestic violence among women in West Bengal. Here all the variables that are significantly associated with domestic violence victimisation in the bivariate analysis ($p <0.01$) have been incorporated into the model and the potential covariates based on the theoretical framework (age, educational qualification, working status, etc.). The multivariate analysis is used to assess the statistical significance of those associations. The adjusted odds ratio (aOR) has been obtained and represented with a 95% confidence interval (CI) and p-values. No multicollinearity has been observed among the independent variables. The relative risk ratios (RRR) with 95% CI and p-values have been reported in the analysis part. SPSS 20.0 software has been used to perform all the statistics.

Critical Analysis

Experiences of Domestic Violence: Types and Severities

The prevalence of diversified forms of domestic violence experienced by the studied respondents indicates that around 69.68% of respondents had experienced domestic violence in their lifetime, with 77.4% having experienced it in the past 12 months (Table 5.1). The forms of domestic violence they had experienced in the past 12 months comprised physical abuse (11.0%), emotional abuse (36.7), both physical and emotional abuse (21.8), and forced sex and substance use (8.0%). The main perpetrators involved in domestic violence were intimate partners (present or former husband) (33.9), in-laws (32.1), and others (husband's relatives, family members) (11.5%).

The association between types of domestic violence experienced by the respondents and perpetrators engaged revealed that violence types significantly varied per perpetrators (Table 5.2). Violence by intimate partners mostly constituted physical abuse (88.4%), followed by both physical and emotional abuse (66%) and forced sex and use of substances like alcohol and drugs (58.0%). Similarly, emotional abuse is mostly perpetrated by in-laws (68.8%), followed by both physical and emotional abuse (27.1%). Again, the most prevalent forms of domestic violence perpetrated by others (husband's relatives, family members) were forced sex and substance use (42.0%),

Table 5.1 Pervasiveness of Domestic Violence among the Respondents

Domestic Violence Experiences	Total N	n (%)
Ever experience of DV in lifetime	1,240	864 (69.68)
Experience of domestic violence in the past 12 months	864	669 (77.4)
Type of violence experienced in the past 12 months	669	
Physical abuse		95 (11.0)
Emotional abuse		317 (36.7)
Both physical and emotional abuse		188 (21.8)
Forced sex and substance use (alcohol, drugs)		69 (8.0)
Main perpetrators of violence in the past 12 months	669	
Intimate partner (current or former husband)		290 (33.6)
In-laws		277 (32.1)
Others (husband's relatives, family members)		102 (11.8)
Frequencies of experiencing domestic violence		
Very often (once a week or two to three times in a month)	669	147 (21.97)
Often (once or twice in a month or two)		270 (40.36)
Occasionally (once or twice in four to six months)		188 (28.10)
Very infrequently (two to three times in a year)		64 (9.57)
Severity of injury	669	
Physically injured but did not require medical care		342 (51.12)
Bruises, deeply wounded but not take any medical care		153 (22.87)
Required medical treatment at home		127 (18.98)
Hospitalised		47 (7.03)

Source: Author computation.

followed by emotional abuse (18.0%). In comparison to women violated by in-laws and others, women violated by intimate partners were significantly more likely to have experienced physical violence (88.4% versus 8.4% and 3.2%, respectively, $p < 0.001$), both physical and emotional violence (66.0% versus 27.1% and 6.9%, respectively, $p < 0.001$), and forced sex and substance use (58.0% versus 0.0% and 42.0%, respectively, $p < 0.001$). Furthermore, women who had been victimised by in-laws were significantly more likely to have experienced emotional abuse compared to women violated by intimate partners and others (68.8% versus 13.2% and 18.0%, respectively, $p < 0.001$).

The frequency of experiences of domestic violence by the respondents in the past 12 months ranges from 21.97% 'very often,' 40.36% 'often,' 28.10% 'occasionally,' and 9.57% 'very infrequently' (Table 5.1). As experiences of domestic violence is a very recurrent behaviour, henceforth the respondents were asked to report how often the perpetrators used violence against them. Of the respondents who have responded being experiencing domestic violence 'very often,' 36.05% faced violence once a week, and 63.95% experienced it twice or thrice in a month. The frequency of experiences of domestic violence once or twice in a month or two was 40.36%, once or twice in four to six months was 28.10%, and twice or thrice in a year was 9.57%. Thus, it divulged

Table 5.2 Comparison of Types of Domestic Violence Experiences among Women and Perpetrators Engaged in the Past 12 Months ($N = 669$)

Violence Type	Perpetrators		
	Intimate Partner	*In-laws*	*Others*
Physical abuse	84 (88.4)	8 (8.4)	3 (3.2) ***
Emotional abuse	42 (13.2)	218 (68.8)	57 (18.0) ***
Both physical and emotional abuses	124 (66.0)	51 (27.1)	13 (6.9) ***
Forced sex and substance use (alcohol, drugs)	40 (58.0)	0 (0.0)	29 (42.0) ***

Notes: Values are numbers of subjects (%). Chi-square test and Phi and Cramer's V have been performed. ***$p < 0.001$
Source: Author computation.

the serious nature of violence in around 62.33% of cases and the trivial nature in roughly 29.67% of cases. Most of the physical abuse happens in the form of kicking, slapping, pulling, pushing, tearing hair, punching, hitting with objects, attempting to suffocate, and so on. Around 28.57% of the battered respondents conveyed being physically mistreated by their husbands occasionally with fists, beaten by hard objects such as sticks or whatever is handy. Around 39.29% of them conveyed that their intimate partners sometimes used to hit them with their hands and sometimes kicked, pushed, or shoved them. About 9.52% of respondents reported that their partners occasionally showed extremely violent attitudes and attempted to suffocate them. About 8.4% of the battered women conveyed that their in-laws used to physically mistreat them. The brutality of domestic violence can be measured by the level of injury. Although physical injuries are easy to measure, it is most difficult to measure the severity of violence in psychological terms. From the intensive fact-finding interview, it has been illustrated that about 51.12% of spousal abuse resulted in physical injury but did not require medical treatment. Around 22.87% of physical abuse resulted in bruises, 18.98% required medical care at home, and 7.03% needed to be hospitalised owing to severe physical injury.

Differentials of Domestic Violence by Background Characteristics

The differentials of domestic violence among the ever-married women who had been mistreated physically, sexually, and emotionally in the past 12 months by background characteristics are represented in Appendix 8. Findings reveal that women belonging to younger age groups (15–18 and 19–29) have experienced more domestic violence in the past 12 months in comparison to older age groups. Women's educational attainment also makes a substantial difference concerning victimisation of violence in domestic environment.

Illiterate women or women who completed primary education have only been found to experience more domestic violence compared to women educated at secondary and higher secondary levels and graduate and above. Women who had married at an early age have experienced more domestic violence in their lives in comparison to women married above 25 years of age. This is perhaps due to their lack of self-reliance, low self-power to confront violence, limited awareness about legal aid, and so on. Again, it has been observed that the prevalence of domestic violence differs by the community of origin of the victims. Women in rural communities have experienced more domestic violence compared to those living in urban communities. This study also revealed that working women, especially those who have been engaged in salaried jobs, have experienced less domestic violence in the past 12 months compared to housewives and self-employed women. Considering the economic condition of families, it can be observed that women belonging to lower and medium economic classes faced more domestic violence in the past 12 months than women belonging to higher economic classes. In the patriarchal culture, it is generally believed that women not bearing children or not having a son are the key causes for domestic violence against women. Here the findings also reveal that respondents having no child or having daughter(s) only (95.6% and 95.8%, respectively) experienced more domestic violence compared to women having only son child or having both son and daughter. It is further reflected in the result that household head sex plays a significant impact in the victimisation of domestic abuse among ever-married women. About 86.6% of women with male-headed households had experienced domestic violence in the past 12 months than female-headed households. Interestingly, most of the battered women (88.8%) considered domestic violence to be justified. Women who had no knowledge of existing legal aids and never confronted violence faced more domestic violence in the past 12 months in comparison to others (97.8% and 96.5%, respectively). The Cronbach's alpha and KMO values for creating composite indicators of 'women justifying domestic violence' are 0.971 and 0.937, respectively, indicating good internal consistency and satisfiable sampling adequacy. The Cronbach's alpha and KMO values for the composite indicator 'confronting domestic violence' also represented good internal consistency and acceptable sampling adequacy (0.958 and 0.861, respectively).

Factors Associated with Domestic Violence Victimisation in West Bengal

The strength of the association of the determinants concerning domestic violence victimisation among the respondents is represented through the results of ODDs ratio obtained from binary logistic regression (Appendix 9). Taking all the socio-demographic variables in one model (gross effects), the findings summarised that the model is strongly correlated with victimisation of domestic violence and it explains 82% of the studied phenomena. Considering the individual effects, it also visualised a strong interlinkage of the determinants with domestic violence victimisation. After controlling the effects of other variables, younger women (15–18 and 19–29 years) are 4.5 (CI: [2.697, 7.400]; p <0.001) and 3.4 (CI: [2.005, 5.599]; p <0.001) times more likely to experience domestic violence compared to the older age groups, respectively. Lower educational attainment leads to a higher possibility of victimisation of domestic violence. This is obvious from the result that illiterate or primary-level educated women and women with secondary and higher secondary educational level are 89.3 (CI: [37.225, 214.072]; p <0.001) and 16.4 (CI: [7.068, 37.907]; p <0.001) times more likely to experience domestic violence in the past 12 months in comparison to graduation and above educational qualifications, respectively. Thus, women's educational qualifications have proven to be one of the main determinants of domestic violence victimisation. Regarding age at marriage, it has been exhibited that women who marry at a younger age (up to 18 years) are 256.8 times (CI: [101.61, 648.83]; p <0.001) more likely to be victimised by domestic violence compared to women who marry at age 25 and above. This may be due to the fact that the higher the age of marriage, the more the maturity and more aware of legal aids, thereby diminishing the possibility of becoming a victim of domestic violence. For the community of origin, the result exhibits that women belonging to urban areas are 73% (aOD .271, CI: [.193, .379]; p <0.001), less likely to victimise domestic violence than rural women. Furthermore, controlling the effects of other variables, it is reflected that housewives and self-employed women are 1.63 (CI: [1.118., 2.371]; p <0.05) and 2.12 (CI: [1.389, 3.228]; p <0.001) times more likely to face domestic violence in comparison to working women, respectively. Again, it is noticed that women belonging to lower and middle economic status are 7.4 (CI: [4.704, 11.659]; p <0.001) and 2.5 times (CI: [1.647, 4.064]; p <0.001) more likely to experience domestic violence as compared to higher economic status, respectively. Regarding the sex of children, women having son child are less likely to experience domestic violence. This is apparent from the result of logistic regression that those women having no child or having daughter(s) only are 19.2 (CI: [9.699, 37.930]; p <0.001) and 40.7 (CI: [20.387, 81.016]; p <0.001) times more likely to experience domestic violence with respect to women having son child only. No significant linkages have been found in-between domestic violence victimisation and women having both son(s) and daughter(s). With respect to households' head sex, women belonging to male-headed households are more likely to experience domestic violence (aOR 2.197, CI: [1.589, 3.036]; p <0.001) than female-headed households. Significant associations have also been found in-between women's views to justify domestic violence and the experiences of being tortured by their present or former husbands. It is manifested from the result of the odds ratio that women who agreed that wife-beating is justified are 2.71 times (CI: [1.827, 4.062]; p<0.001) more likely to victimise domestic violence than those who never accept such thoughts. Likewise, the result is consistent in accordance with the women's knowledge and perceptions about the existing legal provisions. It is noticed that women who have proper knowledge about legal provisions and women's rights or women who are to some extent aware of it are 98% (aOD 0.399, CI: [.265, .602]; p<0.001) and 60% (aOD 0.016, CI: [.008, .032]; p<0.001) less likely to experience domestic violence compared to women having no perceptions about legal aids respectively. And with regards to confront of domestic violence, women who never acquire courage to confront the perpetrator(s) and/or occasionally oppose are more likely to victimise domestic violence in comparison to women who always confront (aOD 22.022 [CI: 12.617, 38.439]; p <0.001; and aOD 8.603 [CI: 4.787, 15.460]; p<0.001).

Discussions

The above study reveals that victimisation of domestic violence amongst women in West Bengal is very much prevalent regardless of all socio-economic status. By analysing the information gathered from in-depth interviews, FGDs, and various secondary data sources, an in-depth understanding of the types, severity, magnitude, and significant determinants of domestic violence victimisation among women in West Bengal has been obtained. The study findings reveal that around 69.68% of the study respondents had experienced some form of domestic violence in their lifespan of whom 77.4% had experienced it in the past 12 months. Physical abuse, emotional abuse, forced sex, and substance abuse were the most common forms of violence they have experienced in a domestic environment in the past 12 months. The perpetrators involved in domestic violence were comprised of intimate partners, in-laws, husband's relatives, or other family members. The responses (both from interviews with the respondents and FGDs with the stakeholders) and the secondary information support to exhume the significant socio-demographic, sociocultural, and situational determinants are highly associated with experiences of domestic violence among the ever-married women in West Bengal. Inverse relationships have evolved with the occurrence of domestic violence and the determinants of women's age, education, age at marriage, standard of living, decision-making power, and courage to confront violence. Lessening the above-mentioned indicators resulting in the prevalence of physical, emotional, and sexual maltreatment among ever-married women in the domestic environment, it is assumed by the male-dominated society that having limited educational attainment may lower self-esteem, make women introverted, ignorant about legal provisions, their rights, and they will suffer battering silently however it may fierce. In the patriarchal society of West Bengal, women are supposed to fulfil all their marital duties. If she fails, it is supposed to be disrespect shown towards the family and ill-treating her is the ultimate way to keep her on the right track. Moreover, in West Bengal's society, less empowerment of women in decision-making in the family is also a significant determinant of experiences of violence in the domestic environment. These observations might be consistent with many other similar research findings that have found close associations between these above-mentioned socio-demographic indicators and the experience of domestic violence (Haque et al., 2022; Sahoo & Pradhan, 2009; Grant, 2007; Semahegn et al., 2013; Kelmendi, 2015; Kwagala et al., 2013; Mootz et al., 2018).

Need for Change: Recommended Measures

Domestic violence against women is unfortunately a grim reality of Indian society. Specifically, marital violence is very much predominant in Indian society; crosses all boundaries of social class, caste, race, and age groups; and is surreptitiously concealed behind closed doors. It is challenging to ascertain the extent of domestic violence incidences as it is happening irrespective of rural areas, towns, cities, and metropolitans as well and often goes unreported. Hence, the Indian government stressed on enacting strong legislative provisions that directly work to prevent and protect women's rights and safeguard them from being victimised by domestic violence. Besides national-level initiatives, the West Bengal state government has also undertaken many measures for the safeguard of women. A separate statutory body, namely the West Bengal Commission for Women, has also been formed for extenuating all forms of violations against women in Bengal. The state government has stressed on setting up many women's police stations across the state so that battered women feel free to report cruelties. Priorities have been given to introducing an online FIR registration portal, more use of modern information technology: mobile applications, social networking platforms for reporting violence, establishing Women Grievance Cells, allotting protection officers at each block, providing free legal services, medical care facilities, and so on. Moreover, for the safety of women from victimisation of domestic violence and provide necessary support to the victims, the state government also collaborates with some NGOs, namely Swayam, the Institute of Social Network (ISN), All Bengal Women's Union, Mahila Seva Samity, and many other self-help groups. Still, West Bengal is witnessing spurt of incidences of domestic violence against women in recent past. The last few consecutive NCRB statistics reflect that West Bengal ranks at the top in terms of domestic violence against women. Though it reflects a positive sign that the reporting rate in West Bengal is presently on the rise, still a huge gap has been noticed in-between the incidence reported and the conviction rates. As per NCRB Report, during 2015, cases convicted under Sec. 498-A IPC in West Bengal were only 215 out of total 20,868 cases chargesheeted. So, the strategies need to be more effective and well-organised. It is required to work on improving the traditional societal beliefs and value systems, improvise women's empowerment, and improve capacity-building to prevent domestic violence against women in West Bengal. Here some strategic prevention measures with respect to the Social Ecological Model (SEM) (modified after Bronfenbrenner, 1986) have been recommended (the framework is given in Figure 5.5). As per the theoretical understanding of SEM, domestic violence in West Bengal is a complex phenomenon and might result from an amalgamation of multiple influences. The dynamic interrelationship among individuals, relationships, community, and societal factors put women at high risk of domestic violence victimisation in society. So, to curb domestic violence, this model suggests taking potential measures at each level simultaneously. Considering this, the present study suggests that at the individual level, strategies should be taken for the overall development of women, their attitudes, beliefs, self-esteem, and behavioural patterns. So, stresses should be given on ensuring women's education, empowering them to take part in family decision-making procedures, support to establish self-help groups, Anganwari kendra, allotting money for the development of space-specific small-scale industries, namely 'biri' industry in Murshidabad, Malda, Nadia, North and South Dinajpur districts; 'madur' (mat) industry in Paschim Medinipur district; and so on. At the relationship level, it is necessary to impart knowledge and education among family members, initiate training for good parenting, and undertake other family-focused prevention measures to maintain healthy family relations. At the community level, it is very much needed to bring changes in the crucial orthodox mindsets of patriarchal society. For that, it is necessary to arrange gender perspective training, awareness programmes, ensure proper justice for the victims in the 'salishi sabha' at the block or panchayat level, and introduce mandate rules for lessening gender discrimination in society. At the societal level, initiatives need to be taken to bring changes in the parental attitude towards justification of domestic violence that may surely reduce the numbers of dowry deaths and other forms of cruelties of their daughters in domestic environment. Domestic violence is deep-rooted in Bengal's society. Apart from introducing strict laws, minimisation of domestic violence against women in West Bengal could not be possible if the people in patriarchal society not change their values and attitudes. Prohibition on giving or taking dowry or strict penalty to the batterers is not the ultimate way to prevent all forms of marital violence at domestic environment. So, some structural changes are needed. These above-mentioned measures might help the government to lessen women victimisation at domestic environment, save the young brides after marriage, enhance their self-esteem, and thus help lessening dowry deaths and all forms of domestic violence in the society.

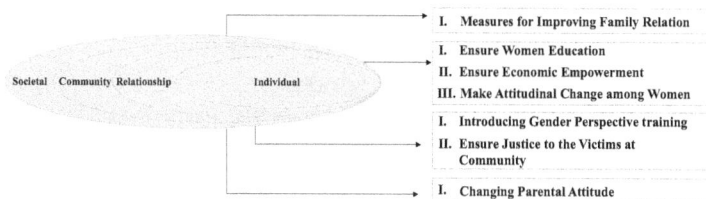

Figure 5.5 Prevention Measures in the Context of the Social Ecological Model

Notes

1 data.gov.in
2 data.gov.in

References

Bronfenbrenner, U. (1986). Ecology of the family as a context for human development: Research perspectives. *Developmental Psychology*, *22*(6), 723.

Chandra, P. S., Satyanarayana, V. A., & Carey, M. P. (2009). Women reporting intimate partner violence in India: Associations with PTSD and depressive symptoms. *Archives of Women's Mental Health*, *12*(4), 203.

Cronbach, L. J. (1951). Coefficient alpha and the internal structure of tests. *Psychometrika*, *16*(3), 297–334. https://doi.org/10.1007/bf02310555. https://link.springer.com/article/10.1007/bf02310555.

Doku, D. T., & Asante, K. O. (2015). Women's approval of domestic physical violence against wives: Analysis of the Ghana demographic and health survey. *BMC Women's Health*, *15*(1), 120.

Falsetti, S. A. (2007). Screening and responding to family and intimate partner violence in the primary care setting. *Primary Care: Clinics in Office Practice*, *34*(3), 641–657.

Garcia-Moreno, C., Jansen, H. A., Ellsberg, M., Heise, L., & Watts, C. H. (2006). Prevalence of intimate partner violence: Findings from the WHO multi-country study on women's health and domestic violence. *The Lancet*, *368*(9543), 1260–1269.

Garcia-Moreno, C., & Stöckl, H. (2009). Protection of sexual and reproductive health rights: Addressing violence against women. *International Journal of Gynecology & Obstetrics*, *106*(2), 144–147.

Golding, J. M., & Taylor, D. L. (1996). Sexual assault history and premenstrual distress in two general population samples. *Journal of Women's Health*, *5*(2), 143–152.

Grant, H. (2007). *Escape domestic violence*. Hodder Arnold.

Haque, M. A., Choudhury, N., Ahmed, S. M. T., Farzana, F. D., Ali, M., Rahman, S. S., Faruque, A. S. G., Raihan, M. J., & Ahmed, T. (2022). Factors Associated with Domestic Violence in Rural Bangladesh. *Journal of Interpersonal Violence*, *37*(3–4), 1248–1269. https://doi.org/10.1177/0886260520922353

Heise, L., Ellsberg, M., & Gottemoeller, M. (1999). Ending violence against women. *Population Reports*, *27*(4).

Kelmendi, K. (2015). Domestic violence against women in Kosovo: A qualitative study of women's experiences. *Journal of Interpersonal Violence*, *30*(4), 680–702.

Khan, M. E., Townsend, J. W., Sinha, R., & Lakhanpal, S. (1996). Sexual violence within marriage. *Seminar-New Delhi, Population Council*, 32–35.

Krantz, G., & Garcia-Moreno, C. (2005). Violence against women. *Journal of Epidemiology & Community Health*, *59*(10), 818–821. https://doi.org/10.1136/jech.2004.022756

Kwagala, B., Wandera, S. O., Ndugga, P., & Kabagenyi, A. (2013). Empowerment, partner's behaviours and intimate partner physical violence among married women in Uganda. *BMC Public Health*, *13*(1), 1–10.

Likert, R. (1932). A technique for the measurement of attitudes. *Archives of Psychology, 22*(140), 1–55.

Miller, J. (2006). A specification of the types of intimate partner violence experienced by women in the general population. *Violence Against Women, 12*(12), 1105–1131.

Mootz, J. J., Muhanguzi, F. K., Panko, P., Mangen, P. O., Wainberg, M. L., Pinsky, I., & Khoshnood, K. (2018). Armed conflict, alcohol misuse, decision-making, and intimate partner violence among women in Northeastern Uganda: A population level study. *Conflict and Health*, *12*(1), 1–11.

National Crime Records Bureau (NCRB). (2018). *Crime in India report*. Retrieved March 3, 2020. https://ncrb.gov.in/

Peltzer, K., & Pengpid, S. (2014). Female genital mutilation and intimate partner violence in the Ivory Coast. *BMC Women's Health*, *14*(1), 13.

Sahoo, H., & Pradhan, M. R. (2009). Domestic violence in India: An empirical analysis. *New Delhi: INDE: Serials*, *89*, 303–321.

Sarkar, N. N. (2008). The impact of intimate partner violence on women's reproductive health and pregnancy outcome. *Journal of Obstetrics and Gynaecology*, *28*(3), 266–271.

Semahegn, A., Belachew, T., & Abdulahi, M. (2013). Domestic violence and its predictors among married women in reproductive age in Fagitalekoma Woreda, Awi zone, Amhara regional state, North Western Ethiopia. *Reproductive Health*, *10*(1), 1–9.

Stephenson, R., Jadhav, A., & Hindin, M. (2013). Physical domestic violence and subsequent contraceptive adoption among women in rural India. *Journal of Interpersonal Violence*, *28*(5), 1020–1039.

Teddlie, C., & Yu, F. (2007). Mixed methods sampling: A typology with examples. *Journal of Mixed Methods Research*, *1*(1), 77–100.

Tjaden, P. G., & Thoennes, N. (2000). *Full report of the prevalence, incidence, and consequences of violence against women: Findings from the National Violence Against Women Survey*. US Department of Justice, Office of Justice Programs, National Institute of Justice.

UNICEF. (2000). *Domestic violence against women and girls*. Innocenti Digest 6. UNICEF Innocenti Research Center.

World Health Organization (WHO). (1997). Violence against women: A priority health issue. *Family and Reproductive Health*. World Health Organization, Geneva.

World Health Organization (WHO). (2013). *Global and regional estimates of violence against women: Prevalence and health effects of intimate partner violence and non-partner sexual violence*. Author.

World Health Organization (WHO). (2017). *Violence against women*. Retrieved March 23, 2020, from www.who.int/news-room/fact-sheets/detail/violence-against-women

6 Application of Geovisual Analytic Tool for Space–Time Visualisation of Crime Compositions and Delineation of Future Potential Areas of Crime Using Statistical Techniques

Introduction

With the rising academic interest in space-based criminological theories since the late twentieth century, a large section of criminological literature has started to discuss the interrelationship between spatial locations and criminogenic events (Anselin et al., 2000). Crime analyses cover a wide range of topics such as delineating crime hotspots (Chainey & Ratcliffe, 2005; Eck et al., 2005; Wu & Grubesic, 2010); determining the underlying built environment that eventually accounts for spatial patterns of crime concentration (Gorman et al., 2001); understanding theoretical context, that is, how specific space exerts influences on the crime patterns (Messner & Anselin, 2004); developing improved methodologies for better understanding of crime data (Levine, 2006; Bernasco & Elffers, 2010); and establishing effective models for legitimate prevention programmes (Ratcliffe, 2004a). Criminogenic study entices considerable attention from geographical aspects also. Since the 1830s, the geographical perspective has played a significant role in understanding the occurrence of criminogenic situations and elaboration of crime prevention measures (Guerry, 1833; Harries, 1974). The practitioners in geography consider space as a significant attribute to understand the crime patterns and emphasise space-based policing. The geographic studies of crime have revealed that criminogenic events are not evenly distributed in space (Chainey & Ratcliffe, 2005; Sherman et al., 1989), rather they cluster in small discrete pockets (Ratcliffe, 2004b; He et al., 2017). Yet the empirical evidence has also revealed the significance of space in policing and specifies that space-based study on crime has gained worldwide attention specifically in Western countries (Weisburd et al., 2010). Apart from understanding the spatial distributional patterns of criminogenic activities, consideration of temporal trends of crimes at varying temporal scales is also of critical interest to criminologists (Townsley et al., 2000; Townsley, 2008). Though both

DOI: 10.4324/9781032696058-6

space and time are fundamental attributes of criminogenic understanding, the combination of spatial and temporal dimensions has not yet been given proportionate consideration in place-based criminogenic research, while comparing with the spatial aspects (Townsley, 2008). Yet to make a legitimate crime prevention effective, the temporal evolvement of spatial crime patterns needs to be understood (Jiang et al., 2021). As literature reveals, both stable and unstable crime hotspots simultaneously exist within a specific space or region (Johnson & Bowers, 2008) and when the spatiotemporal scale of measurement decreases, the crime hotspots become more dynamic and less stable (Mohler et al., 2017). And if crime prevention measures are devoted to the dynamic unstable hotspots, this might cause ample wastage of resources, while generating little or no crime deterrence effects. Therefore, in place-based crime research, the practitioners considered both the spatial and temporal dimensions of crime for making effective prevention measures focusing on the use of scarce resources in an efficient way to the target crime. The geography of crime also stresses on understanding the socio-economic aspects of the crime neighbourhood, the context, and the underneath processes that effect the spatial and temporal variations of criminogenic activities (Hagenauer et al., 2011). Henceforth, the present study is going to visualise and analyse the spatiotemporal context of all forms of crime against women in West Bengal, and unrevealing the underlying mechanisms, it will predict the potentially vulnerable areas of crime for policy purpose and make an insightful understanding about the most striking issue of gender-based violence perpetrated in Bengal's society.

Data Processing and Methodological Overview

Datasets

Datasets are gathered from district-wise open government data available at web portal of data.gov.in: 2,95,884 crime incidents were recorded under four crime heads (rape, cruelties by husband and his relatives, dowry deaths, and women trafficking) from 2002 to 2015. As geocoded datasets are not available, 18 districts of West Bengal have been considered (based on 2011 census) as the spatial units along with temporal variations and crime types. Moreover, districts have been considered (or say neighbourhoods) as base units for another three reasons. First, to make a comprehensive understanding of crime patterns across multiple perspectives; second, each district has definite geographical extension that directly support place-based policing and planning efforts, and third, in broad extent, it might be helpful to indicate the overall pertinent factors responsible for different crime patterns as most of the socio-economic information is available at districts level only.

Data Aggregation and Processing

The available crime datasets (of four crime heads) for each district of varying time periods are aggregated into attribute tables and are normalised depending on the analysis task. In each attribute table, a column denotes the record of a spatial unit (e.g., district), while a row indicates attribute (crime) value in a temporal interval. The value for a cell is demarcated as the total number of crimes that occur in that cell, for example, the total number of rape cases recorded in the Darjeeling District in 2005. After the construction of the attribute tables, data normalisation is done based on the analysis task described subsequently.

Analysis Task: Data Normalisation Technique

To understand the temporal evolvement of spatial crime patterns of differential crime heads in Bengal, crime count in each cell in a specific time series has been divided by the total crime count of that time series. So that the value of each cell now becomes a percentage value depicting the proportion of crimes in each time series for a certain district and crime type.

Multivariate Mapping and Space–Time Visualisation of Crime Attributes

After data normalisation is completed, the thematic mapping technique is solely applied to visualise the district-wise spatial variations of each crime head from 2002 to 2015. Simultaneously, parallel coordinate plot (PCP) and heat map are performed to visualise and analyse how each crime has been distributed across varying temporal ranges in different districts and extricate the districts with similar temporal trends more conveniently. In PCP, each row (district or neighbourhood) in the data table is plotted as a line or profile, and each attribute (year-wise recorded crime data) of a row is plotted as a point on that profile. The values in PCP are always set to be normalised; that is, for each point along the X-axis, the minimum value of the corresponding column is set to '0' and the maximum value is set to '100' along the Y-axis. These data visualisation procedures help the researcher to delineate the most vulnerable districts in terms of crime against women and the execution of the best policy measures. Afterwards, principal component analysis (PCA) (Hotelling, 1933) was performed on the available district-wise socio-economic attributes using SPSS 20 version software to extract the most determining factors accountable for the rising susceptibility of the crime-ridden districts in Bengal. The socio-economic attributes that have been considered for conducting PCA comprise district-wise population density, literacy rate, sex ratio, decadal growth rate, number of immigrants, number of non-working population (Census of India, 2011); HPI (Human Poverty Index) (District Statistical Handbook); GDP

(Gross Domestic Product), HDI (Human Development Index) (Department of Statistics and Programme Implementation, WB 2014–15); amenities (*Economic Review*, 2017–2018, published by Department of Planning, Statistics and Programme Monitoring, West Bengal); and school enrolment ratio (District Statistical Handbook, 2011). These socio-economic attributes have been selected after a deep review of the literature on the determination of factors of crime against women in society. VIF (variance inflation factor) and tolerance have been checked to estimate the multicollinearity among the independent variables (Liu et al., 2003). Variables having large VIF (>10) and low tolerance value (<0.1) denote the existence of strong multicollinearity among the variables (Liu et al., 2003). Afterwards, standardised PCR (principal component regression) (Liu et al., 2003) is conducted with a set of uncorrelated principal components (having eigenvalue close to 1 or above) to execute the linear relationships among the independent variables and crime incidences (considering 2015 data only) and get the best-fit equation as per the principle of maximum adjusted R^2 and minimum standard of error estimation. This best-fit equation helps to obtain a suitable predictive model of potentially vulnerable districts with regard to women victimisation in Bengal. Finally, robust discussions have been done in connection with the socio-economic indicators and spatial extension patterns of crime perpetrated against women in Bengal and have drawn the attention of the practitioners to take the best crime prevention measures (recommended in previous chapters) in the potentially crime-ridden districts after considering the situational socio-economic environmental conditions of those areas.

Analysis

Space–Time Geovisualisations of Crime Compositions

This study analyses the temporal evolvement of crime patterns and their differences across space and the different crime types committed against women in West Bengal. Figures 6.1–6.3 show the result of temporal evolvement of spatial extension patterns of crime against women in Bengal, which include a map-matrix, PCP, and a heat map. In the heat map, the rows represent the districts (neighbourhoods), and the columns represent 14-year time periods from 2002 to 2015. Each column in the heat map corresponds to a map in the map-matrix. In other words, the map-matrix and the heat map both reflect the same data from two distinct perspectives, with the former reflecting the spatial as well as spatiotemporal extensions of crime and the latter focusing on revealing the temporal trends. The PCP is used here to visualise clusters of time series, with each axis representing one time period. This kind of visualisation plots multivariate, numerical data (here year-wise recorded crime data is used) and is ideal for delineation of districts (or say neighbourhoods) with similar temporal trends with regard to crime patterns by comparing the profiles to each other and understanding their interrelationship. In Figure 6.1a, the map-matrix exhibits the temporal evolvement of spatial distributional pattern of crime rape (376- IPC) which reflects that from 2002, the districts of North-24 and South-24 Parganas, Murshidabad, Malda, Hooghly, Jalpaiguri, and Cooch Behar are in a susceptible position with a high to very high concentration of occurrence of rape. After 2005, the districts of Malda and Cooch Behar held a moderate position with a slightly decreasing trend. Again, from 2008 to 2013, Malda and Cooch Behar districts reported a high to very high occurrence of rape in Bengal (except from 2011 to 2012, the district of Cooch Behar posited a moderate trend of rape). Afterwards, from 2014 to 2015, again these two districts hold a moderate position regarding reported incidences of rape. For the Bardhaman district, it has been reflected from the map-matrix that from 2002 to 2005 this district faced a high occurrence of rape. Afterwards, from 2006 to 2012, a decreasing trend has been flowed in Bardhaman, and again from 2013 onwards, a rising trend with a high occurrence of rape has been observed. The map-matrix also reflects that the districts of Purba and Paschim Medinipur hold a moderate position concerning the occurrence of rape during this 14-year period.

From the PCP (Figure 6.1b), a closer look at the clusters of districts with regard to temporal trends of rape has been revealed. The districts of North-24 and South-24 Parganas, Hooghly, Kolkata, Murshidabad, Bardhaman, Malda, Uttar Dinajpur, Cooch Behar, and Jalpaiguri form a cluster of districts with a constant rising trend of rape since 2002–2015. Contrary to these, a declining trend has been observed in the districts of Bankura, Purulia, and Dakshin Dinajpur, with more rape in earlier times compared to later. Similarly, the heat map (Figure 6.1c) reflects the temporal evolvement of district-wise spatial extension patterns of rape since 2002, from which it can also be visualised that the districts of Murshidabad and North-24 and South-24 Parganas are the most vulnerable districts in terms of women safety. Specifically, during 2009 and 2010, Murshidabad witnessed high occurrences of rape incidences; thereafter, they decreased slightly, but the same high pattern continues. In South-24 Parganas, it has been observed that since 2013 there has been a moderate trend of rape cases. It might be due to the initiation of strong legislative measures in the wake of the brutal '*Delhi Nirvaya gang-rape and murder*' incidence.

An obvious temporal evolvement of the spatial distributional pattern of cruelties by the husband or his relatives (498-A IPC) is shown in Figure 6.2. The map-matrix (Figure 6.2a) reveals that since 2002, the districts of North-24 and South-24 Parganas, Hooghly, Howrah, Nadia, Murshidabad, Bardhaman, and Purulia have been witnessing high to very high occurrences of domestic violence against women in Bengal. For the district of Jalpaiguri, a moderate trend has been noticed throughout the time span, although in 2008, 2011, and 2012 a mounting trend with high occurrences of domestic violence was observed in this district. Initially, for 2002 and 2003, a high occurrence of

A. Map-Matrix: Temporal Trends of Rape (376 IPC) Across Space

B. Parallel Coordinates Plot for 376 IPC

C. Heat Map For 376 IPC

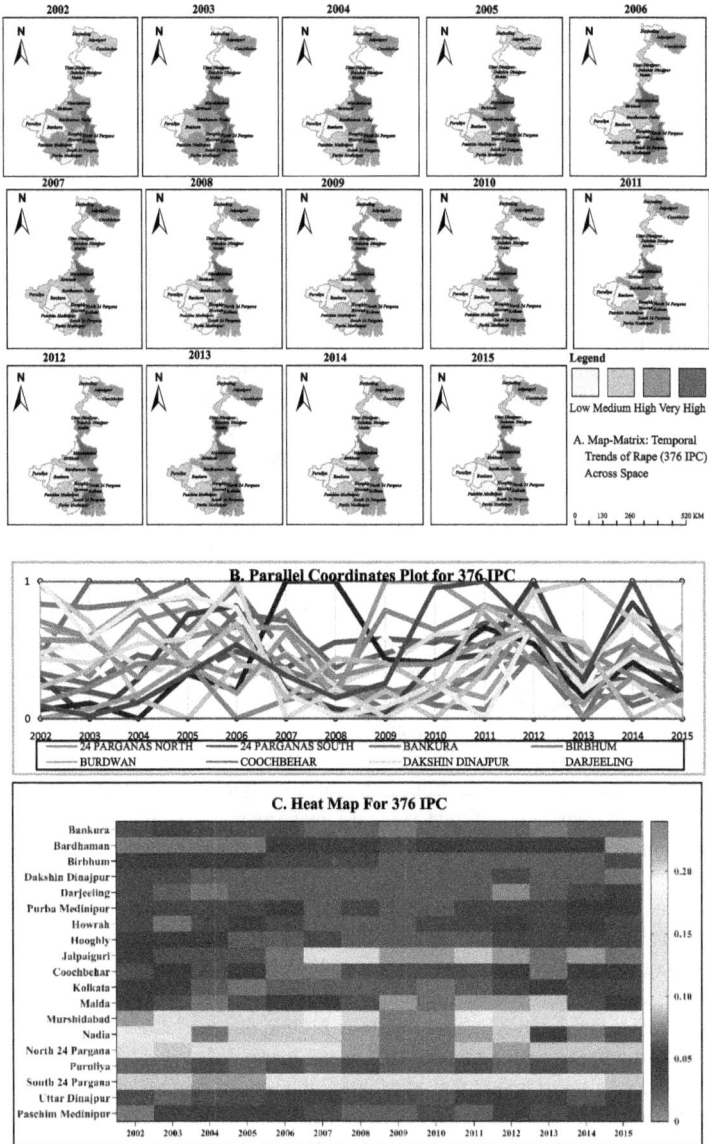

Figure 6.1 Temporal Evolvement of Spatial Extension Patterns of Rape (376 IPC) in West Bengal. (a) Map-matrix. (b) PCP. (c) Heat Map

Source: data.gov.in (2002–2015)

domestic violence victimisation was observed in Paschim Medinipur district. Thereafter, a moderate pattern with relatively less occurrence of incidences (except in 2011) has been observed in this district. From the map-matrix (Figure 6.2a), it is also observed that from 2002 to 2009, the district of Uttar Dinajpur has been witnessing very low occurrences of domestic violence; nonetheless, after 2009, a moderately rising trend has been observed in this district. Besides, very low occurrences of domestic violence have been observed in the districts of Birbhum, Bankura, Dakshin Dinajpur, and Darjeeling, as revealed by the same map-matrix. The PCP (Figure 6.2b) exhibits that the districts of North-24 and South-24 Parganas, Kolkata, Howrah, Purba Medinipur, Uttar Dinajpur, Dakshin Dinajpur, Nadia, and Malda followed a thoroughly rising trend since 2002, with more cases registered in latter times than earlier time periods. In South-24 Parganas, a steadily rising and declining trend with regard to domestic violence (498-A IPC) victimisation has been noticed till 2010. After a sharp decline trend observed up to 2013, domestic violence in this district has risen again. In the district of Malda, incidences of domestic violence followed an unceasingly upheaving trend until 2005 and then declined slightly. From 2007 onwards, there has been a steadily rising trend in this district. The districts of Hooghly, Murshidabad, Cooch Behar, and Darjeeling also followed a steadily rising and falling trend throughout this 14-year time span. The heat map (Figure 6.2c) also reveals the temporal evolvement of spatial extension patterns of 498-A IPC cases, from which it is also observed that the districts of North-24 and South-24 Parganas, Howrah, Nadia, Murshidabad, and Purulia are the most crime-ridden districts in domestic violence victimisation among women, and surprisingly the districts of North-24 and South-24 Parganas and Purulia witnessed maximum incidences of domestic violence from 2013 onwards. It might reflect positive sign as after the amendment of the Criminal Law (Amendment) Act, 2013, awareness among women is increasing, which results in the manifestation of an increasing rate of reporting.

The temporal evolvement of incidences of dowry deaths (304-B IPC) across West Bengal has clearly been illustrated in Figure 6.3. The map-matrix (Figure 6.3a) reflects that the districts of Nadia, Murshidabad, North-24 and South-24 Parganas, and Bardhaman are on the foremost positions in terms of occurrences of dowry deaths since 2002. Earlier, the district of Purba Medinipur had witnessed high to very high occurrences of dowry deaths, although the official figures reveal that after 2010, the severity has declined slightly. For the district of Purulia, it can be noticed that a very minimum number of cases of dowry deaths have been registered officially. It might be due to the reporting rate getting low. It is evident in Figure 6.2 that in Purba Midnapore and Purulia, the number of cases registered under Section 498-A IPC is quite high. So, a big question is being raised about the non-reporting of dowry deaths cases in these two districts. The extreme unawareness about legal aids and the fear of social stigmas possibly force the women and their

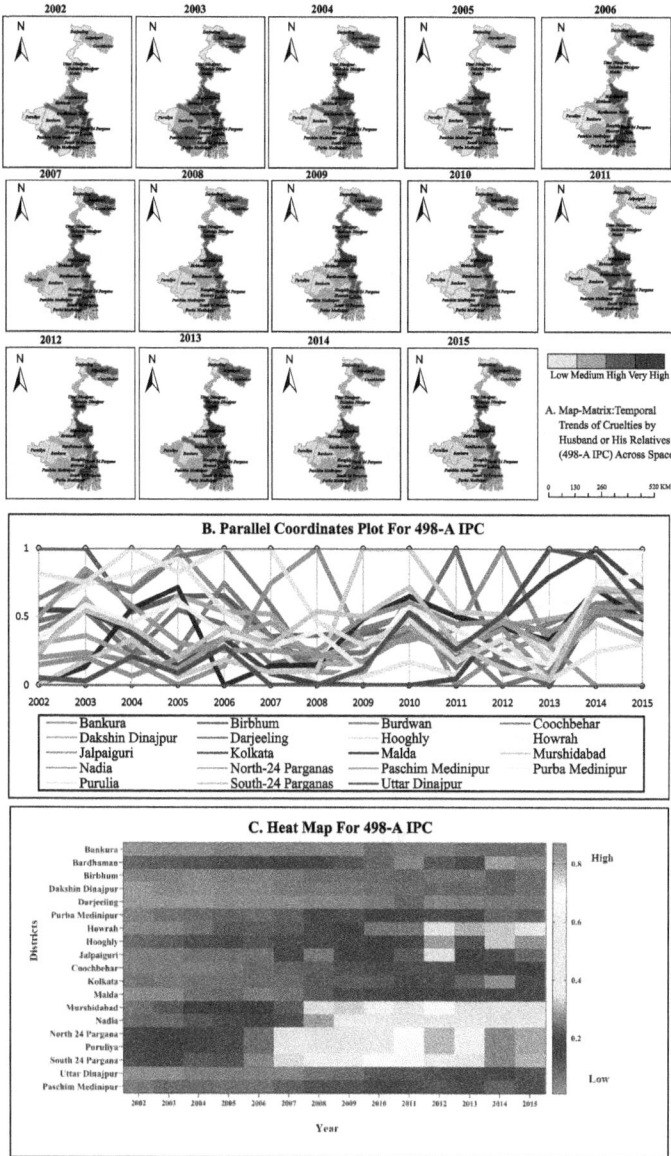

Figure 6.2 Temporal Evolvement of Spatial Extension Patterns of Cruelties by Husband or His Relatives (498-A IPC) in West Bengal. (a) Map-matrix. (b) PCP. (c) Heat Map

Source: data.gov.in (2002–2015)

families to endure inhumane physical and mental torture for high demand of dowry behind closed doors. Contrary to highly vulnerable districts, the same map-matrix also revealed the relatively less or moderately vulnerable districts since 2002 with regard to dowry death cases, which include Darjeeling, Cooch Behar, Jalpaiguri, Uttar and Dakshin Dinajpur, Bankura, Kolkata, Howrah, and Hooghly. The PCP (Figure 6.3b) reveals that the districts of Nadia, Hooghly, Malda, and Cooch Behar form a cluster with continuous rising trend since 2002. Another form of similar distributional patterns with steady rising and falling trend of dowry deaths since 2002 has been observed in the districts of Bardhaman, Birbhum, Darjeeling, and Uttar and Dakshin Dinajpur. Since 2012, a gradual decreasing trend in these districts has been observed. In North-24 and South-24 Parganas, Purba Medinipur, and Bankura, it follows an average temporal pattern with less dowry deaths cases registered in latter periods. In the state capital Kolkata, it also follows a somewhat rising trend during this time span. The temporal evolutionary patterns of dowry deaths (304-B IPC) across districts are evidently reflected in the heat map (Figure 6.3c). From this, it can be observed that more or less all the districts in West Bengal have been witnessing many incidences of dowry deaths during this 14-year time-span. The most vulnerable districts with high to very high occurrences of dowry deaths since 2002 are North-24 and South-24 Parganas, Murshidabad, Nadia, and Bardhaman. In South-24 Parganas, it has been reflected from the heat map that initially, a very high trend of dowry deaths has been observed, but later the rate decreased slightly, although it followed a higher to moderately higher trend. In North-24 Parganas, since 2004, a considerably higher trend of dowry deaths has been observed, although after 2010 onwards the number has increased dramatically. Since 2002, a moderate to high trend of dowry deaths in Bardhaman has been clearly reflected from the same heat map.

So, the entire space–time visualisation illustrates that throughout West Bengal, the incidences of rape and sexual harassment, domestic violence, and dowry deaths are inheritably deep-rooted in society. The concentration is high in some specific districts, namely North-24 and South-24 Parganas, Murshidabad, Nadia, Hooghly, Bardhaman, Cooch Behar, Malda, and East Medinipur. Moreover, differential spatial distributional patterns of different forms of crimes have evolved from the official data. That means not all crimes are equally concentrated in each district. For example, no specific spatial distributional pattern has been noticed for incidences of domestic violence in Bengal. Contrary to this, the districts of North-24 and South-24 Parganas, Murshidabad, Nadia, Bardhaman, and Jalpaiguri have witnessed maximum occurrences of rape and sexual harassment against women in the last decades. Specific spatial concentration of criminogenic events has also been noticed for incidences of acid attacks and trafficking in young women and minor girls in West Bengal. Here it is not possible to arrange proper visualisation of the temporal evolvement of the spatial extension patterns of acid attacks and women

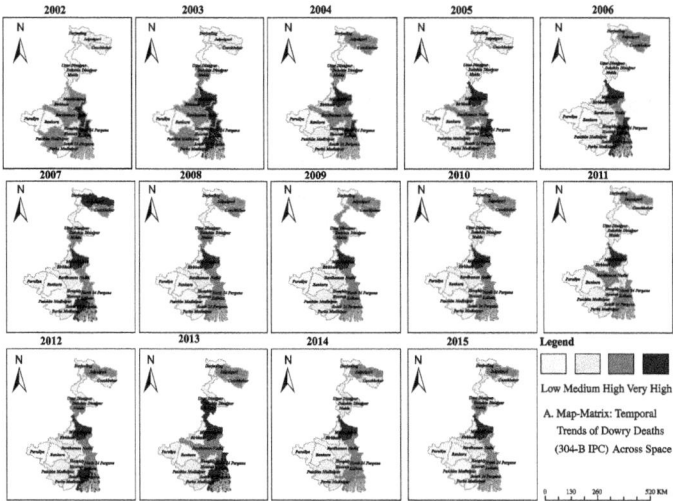

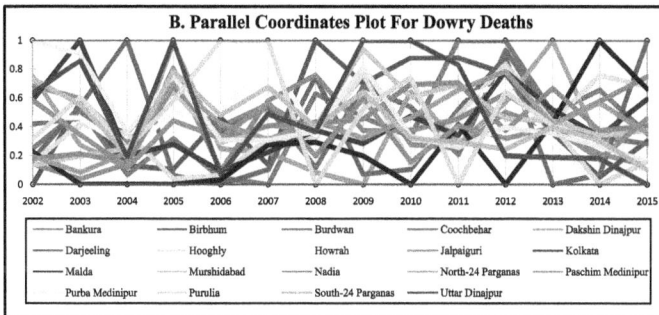

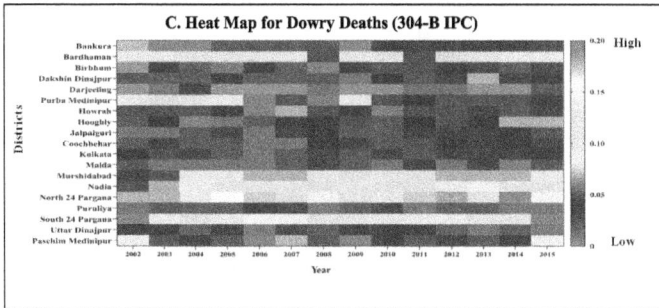

Figure 6.3 Temporal Evolvement of Spatial Extension Patterns of Dowry Deaths (304-B IPC) in West Bengal. (a) Map-matrix. (b) PCP. (c) Heat Map

Source: data.gov.in (2002–2015)

trafficking incidences due to the inaccessibility of district-wise long-term government data. During the detailed study on women trafficking in Bengal (mentioned earlier in Chapter 2), it has been found that trafficking activities are mostly concentrated in the border districts of West Bengal, namely North-24 and South-24 Parganas, Murshidabad, Malda, Nadia, Uttar and Dakshin Dinajpur, Cooch Behar, and Darjeeling. It is also evident (mentioned earlier in Chapter 3) that in South Bengal, the intensity of acid attacks is maximum compared to North Bengal. Now the questions arise that why specific districts are more susceptible to occurrences of crime against women in West Bengal? In previous chapters, detailed discussions about the situational socio-economic and physical environmental backcloths for each form of crime perpetrated against women in West Bengal have been made. This chapter is shedding light to make a comprehensive understanding of the situational criminogenic environment in West Bengal from a holistic perspective.

Understanding the Contextual Settings of Inhomogeneous Crime Concentration

Data Normality

Before performing any statistical modelling, it is worth verifying whether the available data satisfy the underlying distribution assumptions or not? In multivariate statistical techniques, namely PCA, the most frequently made distributional assumption is multivariate normal distribution. An important property of multivariate normal distribution is if $X = (X_1, X_2, \ldots X_n)$, follow the multivariate normal distribution pattern, then all the individual components of $X_1, X_2, \ldots, X_n$ are considered to be normally distributed. So, normality each X_i has to be checked to ensure that $X = (X_1, X_2, \ldots, X_n)$ is multivariate normal distributed. Here quantile–quantile plot (QQ plot) has been used to assess data normality which reveals that all the 11 variables (population density, literacy rate, sex ratio, decadal growth rate, numbers of immigrants, number of non-working population, HPI, GDP, HDI, amenities, and school enrolment ratio) are almost normally distributed.

Result of Principal Component Analysis

To determine the numbers of PCs (principal components), the Kaiser's criterion (Dikko et al., 2013) has been followed. The resulting KMO value of 0.60 with p-value (sig.) <0.05 and the approximate chi-square of 97.974 with 45 degree of freedom (df) reject the null hypothesis (H_0) and accept the alternative hypothesis (H_1) of existence of strong correlation in-between variables (Appendix 10). Henceforth, it stipulates that PCA is the best technique for further analysis of the datasets. The factor loadings of variables (Appendix

11) after varimax rotation with Kaiser normalisation resulting from factor analysis exhibit that all the 11 variables are grouped into 4 major PCs with eigenvalue greater than 1, which explain 80.86% of the total variables. The PCs are labelled as socio-economic adversity and disorganisation; population inflow, gender imparity, and social disorganisation; socio-demographic indicators and emerging issues; and lack of basic amenities and consequence social disorder, respectively.

The scree plot graphically represents the number of PCs to retain. It reflects a sharp change in the curvature after PC 4, which specifies that the first 4 PCs account for 80.86% of the total variance after which the total variance is explained minimum by the remaining PCs.

PCR and Validation

The PCR executes the 'best possible' standardised principal component regression equation to predict the relative contributions of all the PCs (independent variables) on the outcome variable crime (dependent variable) and delineate the future potentiality of crime in each district of West Bengal based on it.

Validation of the Underlying Assumptions

MEASURES OF MULTICOLLINEARITY

The result of collinearity statistics reveals that both the value of VIF and tolerance are lying within the accepted range. All VIFs are less than 10 and all tolerance values are greater than 0.1, suggesting that no multicollinearity exists in-between the PCs.

MEASURES OF INDEPENDENCE OF RESIDUALS AND OUTLIER ANALYSIS

The Durbin Watson value of 2.208 indicates no violations of the independence of residual assumptions (the rule-of-thumb is that the Durbin Watson value close to 2 denotes independence of residuals assumptions is not violated) (Alawneh et al., 2013). The Cook's distance and cantered leverage values are also in the satisfactory range, denoting that the model is not influenced by the outliers.

Result of Multiple Linear Regression

The model summary shows the result of R, R^2, and F statistics for all the predictor variables in the linear model. The value of $F = 20.121$ ($p < 0.05$) reflects that the model is statistically significant. R^2 represents the goodness of fit of the linear model which depicts that about 86% of the total variance of crime occurrence is explained by the regression equation. Table 6.1 shows the standardised regression coefficient of each predictor. It reflects that the PC 1 (socio-economic adversity and disorganisation), PC 2 (population inflow, gender imparity, and social disorganisation), and PC 4 (lack of basic amenities and consequence social disorder) are the predictors that significantly (p <0.05, p <0.01, and p <0.05, respectively) predict the occurrences of crime against women in West Bengal. However, the regression result reveals that PC 3 (socio-demographic indicators and emerging issues) made no significant (p >0.05) influences on crime against women in Bengal. It can be overviewed from the standardised β-coefficient that individually PC 1 explains 32% of the variance, PC 2 explains 68% of the variance, and PC 4 explains 31% of variance of crime. Hence, it can be concluded that 86% of the variance of women victimisation in Bengal is attributed to population inflow, pressure of economy and social disorganisation, gender imparity, illiteracy, poverty, lack of basic amenities, and other socio-economic adversities. Fourteen percent of the variance in crime occurrence in Bengal might be attributed to other factors, namely environmental vulnerabilities and increasing risk factors, improper execution of undertaken policies and legislative measures, and other behavioural and sociocultural determinants.

Table 6.1 Result of Multiple Linear Regression Analysis

Predictors	Coefficients[a]				
	Unstandardised Coefficients		Standardised Coefficient β	t	Sig.
	β	Std. Error			
(Constant)	1666.258	143.892		11.580	.000
Socio-economic adversity and disorganisation	405.674	167.169	.323	2.427	.031*
Population inflow, gender imparity, and social disorganisation	804.956	127.595	.675	6.309	.000**
Socio-demographic indicators and emerging issues	144.850	122.773	.122	1.180	.259
Lack of basic amenities and consequence social disorder	763.936	328.966	.314	2.322	.037*
**p < 0.01, *p < 0.05, [a]Dependent variable: crime against women.					

Source: Author computation.

Determination of Future Potential Hotspots of Crime against Women in West Bengal

After transforming the 'best-fit' standardised principal component regression equation into the standardised linear regression equation: $\hat{y} = a + \beta_1 X_1 + \beta_2 X_2 + \beta_3 X_3 + \beta_4 X_4$ (a = intercept; β_1 = coefficient; X_1, X_2, X_3, X_4 = predictor variables [independent variables]), an apparent predictive model of potentially vulnerable districts of victimisation of crime among women has been obtained (Figure 6.4). It specifies that in near future, the districts of South Bengal, namely

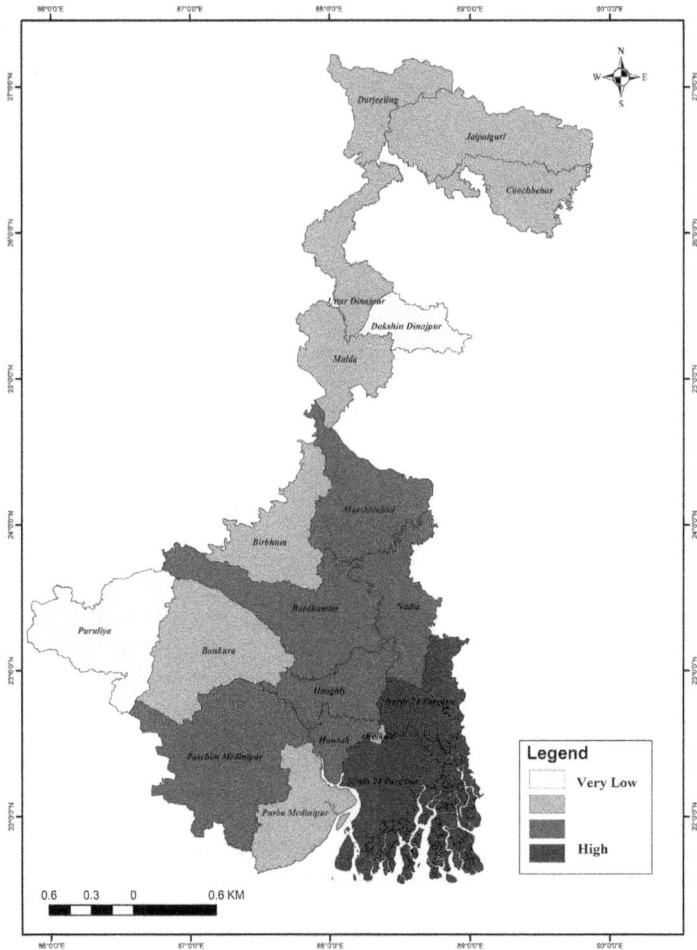

Figure 6.4 Potentially Vulnerable Areas of Crime in West Bengal

North-24 and South-24 Parganas, Nadia, Murshidabad, Howrah, Hooghly, Bardhaman, Paschim Medinipur and Jalpaiguri, Cooch Behar, and North and South Dinajpur of North Bengal are likely to become more vulnerable with regard to rising incidences of crime against women.

Discussions

This chapter exhumes an insightful understanding of the geography of crime against women in West Bengal using multivariate mapping for space–time visualisation to make effective and efficient legitimate crime prevention measures. To understand the occurrence mechanism of criminogenic settings and women susceptibility in West Bengal, this study made an effort to evaluate the temporal evolvement of spatial crime patterns to develop a better understanding of the most vulnerable districts and reveal how specific spaces exert the stimulus socio-economic backcloths that eventually affect the spatiotemporal variations of criminogenic events. The study findings reveal that the crime against women has been deeply rooted throughout West Bengal, irrespective of age, race, socio-economic status, and occupational attainment. Yet, specific spatiotemporal distributional patterns of violations against women have been reflected through the multivariate mapping for space–time visualisation. Specific pockets in Bengal have emerged as hotbeds of crime, enhancing women's susceptibility in those areas. Specifically, the remote villages of Indo-Bangladesh border districts of Bengal have emerged as hotbeds of women trafficking. Every day, many poor minor girls and young women remain missing from the frontier blocks like Sitalkuchi, Sitai, Dinhata I and II, Mekhliganj, Haldibari of Cooch Behar; Bamongola, Kaliachak I and II, Manikchak of Malda; Dhulian, Domekal, Lalgola of Murshidabad; Sandeshkhali I and II, Haroa, Minakhan, and Hingalganj of North-24 Parganas and are trafficked to metros and other corners of India for commercial exploitation. The strategic location of these border districts results in high-level socio-economic disorganisation in society that eventually puts poor women at high risk of being trapped in trafficking. In addition, the extreme socio-economic adversities in the tea estates of North Bengal and the continuous exposure to extreme environmental hazardous situations and consequent socio-economic hostility in the remote riverine villages of the deltaic Sundarbans regions of South Bengal make these areas significant sources as well as transit hubs of women trafficking. Over the past few years, irrespective of rural and urban areas, the districts of North-24 and South-24 Parganas, Hooghly, Murshidabad, Malda, and Jalpaiguri have caused the utmost insecurity among women concerning the victimisation of rape and sexual harassment in West Bengal. From the space–time visualisation, no specific patterns have been observed for the victimisation of violence by women in domestic environments in West Bengal. Yet, the districts of Purba and Paschim Medinipur, Purulia, South-24

Parganas, Kolkata, Howrah, and Hooghly witnessed the maximum reported incidences of 498-A IPC and 304-B IPC; nonetheless, during the intense study, it has been observed that throughout Bengal, irrespective of class, caste, and economic status, women have been experiencing cruelties in their domestic environment. This study executed significant associations ($p < 0.05$) of socio-economic factors with the rising incidences of crime against women in West Bengal and asserted that acute poverty, unemployment, high population inflow, illiteracy, lack of requisite amenities, gender imparity, and other socio-economic adversities attributed to 86% of the variance of women susceptibilities in West Bengal. The apparent predictive model of potential crime hubs in Bengal specifies that the PC1, PC 2, and PC 4 significantly predict ($p < 0.05$, $p < 0.01$, and $p < 0.05$, respectively) that in the near future the districts of North-24 and South-24 Parganas, Hooghly, Howrah, Murshidabad, Nadia, Paschim Medinipur, Bardhaman, North and South Dinajpur, Jalpaiguri, and Cooch Behar might posit the foremost position regarding women susceptibility in West Bengal. Studies also revealed that socio-economic deprivation induced by acute poverty has a strong influence on rising incidences of crime (Debnath & Roy, 2013). Therefore, the concerned government should focus on the abolition of economic deprivation in society by eliminating poverty, opening more employment opportunities to minimise social disorganisation, and restraining the advancement of the criminogenic environment in society. The obvious situational crime prevention measures mentioned separately in earlier chapters of this book should be executed properly by the concerned government to weaken all the influential factors accountable for crime victimisation among women in West Bengal, thus increasing the opportunity cost of the offenders. Given the complexity, differential situational factors, and time-varying nature of different forms of crime against women in West Bengal, the adopted data-driven and exploratory approaches of geovisualisation and statistical techniques are indispensable for understanding crime data and providing timely information for immediate response.

References

Alawneh, A., Al-Refai, H., & Batiha, K. (2013). Measuring user satisfaction from e-government services: Lessons from Jordan. *Government Information Quarterly*, *30*(3), 277–288.

Anselin, L., Cohen, J., Cook, D., Gorr, W., & Tita, G. (2000). Spatial analyses of crime. *Criminal Justice*, *4*(2), 213–262.

Bernasco, W., & Elffers, H. (2010). Statistical analysis of spatial crime data. In A. R. Piquero & D. Weisburd (Eds.), *Handbook of quantitative criminology* (pp. 699–724). Springer.

Census of India. (2011). *Ministry of home affairs*. Government of India.

Chainey, S., & Ratcliffe, J. (2005). *GIS and crime mapping*. John Wiley & Sons.

Debnath, A., & Roy, N. (2013). Linkage between internal migration and crime: Evidence from India. *International Journal of Law, Crime and Justice, 41*(3), 203–212.

Dikko, H., Osi, A. A., & Bello, Y. (2013). Detecting factors impacting crime rates in Nigeria using principal component analysis. *IOSR Journal of Mathematics, 9*(3), 8–17.

District Statistical Handbook. (2011). *Office of the Registrar General & Census Commissioner, India*. Ministry of Home Affairs, Government of India. https://censusindia.gov.in/2011census/dchb/WB.html

Eck, J. E., Chainey, S., Cameron, J. G., Leitner, M., & Wilson, R. E. (2005). *Mapping crime: Understanding hot spots* (NIJ special report). www.ojp.gov/pdffiles1/nij/209393.pdf

Gorman, D. M., Speer, P. W., Gruenewald, P. J., & Labouvie, E. W. (2001). Spatial dynamics of alcohol availability, neighborhood structure and violent crime. *Journal of Studies on Alcohol, 62*(5), 628–636.

Guerry, A. M. (1833). *Essai sur la statistique morale de la France*. Crochard.

Hagenauer, J., Helbich, M., & Leitner, M. (2011). Visualization of crime trajectories with self-organizing maps: A case study on evaluating the impact of hurricanes on spatio-temporal crime hotspots. In *Proceedings of the 25th conference of the International Cartographic Association*, Paris.

Harries, K. D. (1974). *The geography of crime and justice*. McGraw-Hill.

He, L., Páez, A., & Liu, D. (2017). Persistence of crime hot spots: An ordered probit analysis. *Geographical Analysis, 49*(1), 3–22.

Hotelling, H. (1933). Analysis of a complex of statistical variables into principal components. *Journal of Educational Psychology, 24*(6), 417.

Jiang, C., Liu, L., Qin, X., Zhou, S., & Liu, K. (2021). Discovering spatial-temporal indication of crime association (STICA). *ISPRS International Journal of Geo-Information, 10*(2), 67.

Johnson, S. D., & Bowers, K. J. (2008). Stable and fluid hotspots of crime: Differentiation and identification. *Built Environment, 34*(1), 32–45.

Levine, N. (2006). The CrimeStat program: Characteristics, use and audience. *Geographical Analysis, 38*(1), 41–56. https://doi.org/10.1111/j.0016-7363.2005.00673

Liu, R. X., Kuang, J., Gong, Q., & Hou, X. L. (2003). Principal component regression analysis with SPSS. *Computer Methods and Programs in Biomedicine, 71*(2), 141–147.

Messner, S. F., & Anselin, L. (2004). Spatial analyses of homicide with areal data. In M. F. Goodchild & D. G. Janelle (Eds.), *Spatially integrated social science* (Vol. 12, pp. 127–144). Oxford University Press.

Mohler, G. O., Short, M. B., & Brantingham, P. J. (2017). The concentration dynamics tradeoff in crime hot spotting. In D. Weisburd & J. Eck (Eds.),

Unraveling the crime-place connection (Vol. 22, pp. 19–40). Taylor & Francis.

Ratcliffe, J. H. (2004a). Crime mapping and the training needs of law enforcement. *European Journal on Criminal Policy and Research, 10*(1), 65–83.

Ratcliffe, J. H. (2004b). The hotspot matrix: A framework for the spatiotemporal targeting of crime reduction. *Police Practice and Research, 5*(1), 5–23.

Sherman, L. W., Gartin, P. R., & Buerger, M. E. (1989). Hot spots of predatory crime: Routine activities and the criminology of place. *Criminology, 27*(1), 27–56.

Townsley, M. (2008). Visualising space time patterns in crime: The hotspot plot. *Crime Patterns and Analysis, 1*(1), 61–74.

Townsley, M., Homel, R., & Chaseling, J. (2000). Repeat burglary victimisation: Spatial and temporal patterns. *Australian & New Zealand Journal of Criminology, 33*(1), 37–63.

Weisburd, D., Telep, C. W., & Braga, A. A. (2010). *The importance of place in policing: Empirical evidence and policy recommendations* (pp. 1–68). Swedish National Council for Crime Prevention.

Wu, X., & Grubesic, T. H. (2010). Identifying irregularly shaped crime hotspots using a multiobjective evolutionary algorithm. *Journal of Geographical Systems, 12*(4), 409–433.

7 Discussions and Conclusion

Discussions

The present study makes a vivid understanding about the very burning issue of crime against women in West Bengal. Daily newspapers are filled with incidents of dowry deaths, cruelty by husband and his relatives, rape and other forms of sexual abuses, the gruesome incidence of acid attacks, women trafficking, and many other forms of gender-based atrocities. Many adverse physical and psychological health outcomes emerge as consequences of crime against women that ultimately subversive the progress of the society. The gender-based atrocities in West Bengal has reached its maximum over the past decade that raise big concern among the practitioners, policymakers, criminologists, and the social activists about the safety of women in Bengal. The complete spatial variability of crimes against women in West Bengal brings difficulties in perpetuating proper measures to control the victimisation of specific crime types. Many effective measures have already been undertaken by the state government along with the existing legislative provisions mentioned in IPC, yet every day many incidences of rape, child marriage, kidnapping, women trafficking, domestic violence, dowry deaths are often heard. Naturally questions arise: Are there any gaps in-between policy formulation and implementation? Is strengthening the existing laws alone not enough to minimise gender-based oppression in West Bengal? The present criminological understanding not only focuses on individual perpetrator characteristics but also excavates the surrounding environment that eventually drive a person to do illicit activities. The more the environment is disorganised, the greater the likelihood of criminogenic activities in a region. Here by using the term 'environment,' the criminologists refer to both the physical and socioeconomic environment. Therefore, proper understanding about the existing situational environment is highly needed to take the most effective measures to curb any criminological activities in a region. For gender-based issues, the societal stereotype mindsets, specifically the patriarchal thinking nurtured in India, play a substantial role. Henceforth, to curb victimisation among women, it is very much required to consider the conservative attitudes of

DOI: 10.4324/9781032696058-7

society along with the existing socio-economic ecological settings. Besides, in recent days, application of GIS technologies, an analytical tool to visualise complex crime pattern, is very much admissible to the practitioners world-wide to yield space-specific measures to curb oppression. Thus, it is needed to understand how effective the use of GIS technology is in curbing crimes against women in West Bengal. On this ground, the present study has tried to meet all the research questions that evolved during the literature review and focused on understanding the existing scenario and the complex crime patterns in West Bengal. Finally, some strategic situational environmental crime prevention measures have been recommended to inhibit brutalities against women in West Bengal. In this study, four major categories of crime, namely women trafficking, rape and sexual harassment, acid attacks, and domestic violence, have been considered for conducting the in-depth study based on intense literature review and incidences recorded at national- and state-level crime directory.

The entire study has seamlessly explored the existing spatial variability of crime committed against women in West Bengal, steadily excavated the underlying determinants, and critically discussed emerging criminogenic issues on the bases of theoretical understanding and immediate situations. The study reveals that the heinous offence of trafficking in women, acid attacks, rape, eve-teasing, and domestic violence in West Bengal is increasing irrespective of all socio-economic status. The geographical strategic location of West Bengal has an immense role in making specific areas vulnerable to specific criminogenic activities. Certain space-specific factors more precisely say the adverse physical environment sometimes upheaves the socio-economic vulnerabilities in an area and thus results in lamentation of socio-economic imbalances, large-scale social disorganisation, breakdown of social ties, and exacerbates illicit activities in that region. The glimpse of such environmental vulnerabilities and consequent socio-economic hostility and illicit criminal activities in a region can be appraised from the emerging issues of women trafficking in the remote riverine villages of Sundarbans deltaic region of South-24 Parganas and the porous border districts in West Bengal. The hostile physiographic location, lack of basic amenities, unavailability of resources, unfavourable infrastructural set-up, unemployment and pseudo-unemployment, intense poverty, share of porous international borders in addition to constant exposure to natural calamities, sea-level rise, extreme flood situations in the deltaic region of Sundarbans result in large-scale socio-economic imbalances, acute poverty, and homelessness and eventually effect the impoverish groups in society. Such socio-economic hostility put the poor women and minor girls in the deltaic villages of Sundarbans into great threat. The traffickers take advantage of these adverse situational environments and entice the poor women and minors for great job prospects in metros and traffic them. Another notable instance of spatial variability of crime against women in West Bengal can be observed in another form of brutality, that is, acid attacks. This study intensively examines the magnitude of acid attacks against women in Bengal and identifies the major hotspots which reveal that South Bengal is comparatively more vulnerable compared to North Bengal. Canning, Baruipur of South-24 Parganas, Bongaon, Ashok Nagar, Habra, Bagda, Gaighata of North-24 Parganas, Bagnan, Uluberia subdivision of Howrah, Purbasthali of Bardhaman, Ghatal in Paschim Medinipur, and even Kolkata and Hooghly, everywhere such vengeful acts scar the life of young women. This modern revenge strategy against women in Bengal sentenced the young women to a plight worse than death just for rejection of marriage or love proposals, past revenge, domestic violence, and dowry demands. Yet no definite physical, geographic, or environmental illustration could be drawn regarding this spatial pattern of acid violence in West Bengal. Mostly, the sociopsychological determinants of male dominance, desire to take revenge, and illiteracy are accountable for such a ghastly nuisance. Yet if the situational environment is considered, it can be illustrated from this intense study that in South Bengal many gold shops and heavy industries are there. Acid is required for this purpose. Acid is supplied to the battery industries, heavy metal industries, hardware shops, and gold shops of the Kolkata suburban region from the wholesalers in the Barabazar area of Kolkata. Most of the hardware retailers and battery retailers of Kolkata suburban areas have no legal licence, and they deal directly with acid without maintaining any proper registration. And it is so astonishing that in most incidences of acid attacks in the subdivisions of Baruipur, Sonarpur, Ghatal, Uluberia, and Habra of South Bengal, the delinquents worked as gold mechanics, and the hardware shops, battery shops, and grocery shops were also the prime sources of acid in the hands of the culprits. No specific spatial concentration is observed for the very burning issue of rape in Bengal. In the last ten years, an immense jump has been noticed in the incidence of rape in West Bengal. The early 2012 brutal *Park Street (Kolkata) gang-rape case*, the 2013 *Kamduni gang-rape and murder case* (Barasat, North-24 Parganas), the *Madhyamgram gang-rape and suicidal case* (North-24 Parganas), and the 2020 *Kumarganj gang-rape and ablaze death case* (South Dinajpur) are consistently reminiscent of the barbarism of the mediaeval era. Situational environmental factors such as abundant places, absence of formal and informal guardians, and lack of streetlights play a substantial role in many cases of rape and sexual harassment, but this study intensively explores that the societal foster beliefs and attitudes of male superiority are deeply rooted in the patriarchal culture of West Bengal. The rape myths, that is, the victim-blaming attitudes of society, also act as catalysts to upsurging sexual offences against women and induce non-reporting of incidences. In addition to the aforementioned crimes, for centuries, evermarried women in West Bengal, irrespective of all socio-economic strata and educational backgrounds, have been subjected to various forms of abuse in the domestic environment only for orthodox patriarchal societal thoughts. For these gender-based atrocities, no such spatial or geographical variability has been noticed in Bengal. Mostly in the districts of Howrah, North-24 Parganas, Nadia, Jalpaiguri, Murshidabad, Hooghly, Paschim Medinipur, and South-24 Parganas, the reporting rate of domestic violence victimisation among women is very high. Yet from this intense study, it has been revealed that more or less every woman (69.68% of study respondents) throughout Bengal has often experienced any form of domestic violence in their lifetime. The patriarchal culture and the traditional social norms and beliefs practiced in Bengal's society justify women subordination and believe that mistreating women is the best way to keep them in their place. In addition, the socio-demographic determinants, namely women's age, educational status, monetary dependency, male-headed household, decision-making power, justification of violence, lack of knowledge about legal aids, and inability to confront violence, have an immense role in increasing the risk of victimisation among women in the domestic environment in West Bengal.

There are many legislative provisions that have already been mentioned in the IPC and CrPC to prevent and suppress crime against women so that women can move forward with all their inner potential, and thus society would progress. After the frightening incidence of the '2012 Delhi gang-rape case,' numerous new legislations have been incorporated and amendments have been made in the existing IPC and CrPC to strengthen the existing provisions ordered by the apex court. Many fast-track courts and special courts have also been set up by the government for faster investigation and disposal of the cases. The protection of Women from Domestic Violence Act (PWDVA), 2005, has been introduced safeguard women from domestic violence victimisation. The Sexual Harassment of Women at Workplace (Prevention, Prohibition and Redressal) Act, 2013, has also been introduced by the Indian Parliament for the protection of working women at their workplace. In 2018, the Criminal Law (Amendment) Act, 2018, was introduced by the parliament after nationwide protests in the notorious 'Kathua gang-rape and murder case.' This Act stipulates death penalty as a possible punishment for raping a girl under the age of 12. The Supreme Court has issued strict guidelines for the sale of acid in the open market and introduced stringent punishments for those accused of acid attacks. Furthermore, many statutory bodies, namely the National Commission for Women and the Ministry of Women and Child Development, have been already set up by the government of India to protect women's rights. The Indian government has also put in rigorous efforts to address gender–gap issues in society, introduced the *Beti Padhao, Beti Bachao* scheme to lessen violence and ensure women's rights. Apart from these, the state government has also undertaken many initiatives for minimising the risk of violence victimisation among women in Bengal. Many women police stations have been set up across the state. In 2016, the novel initiative 'Swayangsiddha Project' was started by the South-24 Parganas district police, which has achieved great success in combating trafficking in women and preventing early age marriage practices in this district. Several NGOs, namely 'SANLAAP,' 'Goranbose Gram Bikash Kendra (GGBK),' 'Birangana Seva Samity' of Canning subdivision, 'Bandhanmukti,' and 'Uthan,' are rigorously working in collaboration with the government to prevent trafficking in the district. The state government has introduced schemes like '*Kanyashree Prakalpa*' and '*Ruposhree Prakalpa*' to ensure more participation of girls in schools and colleges and prevent underage marriage practice in Bengal. *The Ministry of Women and Children Development and Social Welfare* of West Bengal has been working hard to formulate policies and to secure basic rights of women and minors. Another statutory body *The West Bengal Commission for Women* is also working to mitigate all forms of women issues. Emphasis has been put on improving capacity-building, an online web portal for registering FIRs, Women Grievance Cells, and so on. The Kolkata police have opened their own 'Facebook' page, WhatsApp number, and mobile app named *Bondhu* for the safety of women and children from any forms of atrocities. In addition, initiatives such as self-defence training programmes for young girls and women have been made by the government to make them aware and self-reliant. Despite taking such effective measures both at the central and state levels, crime against women in Bengal has not yet been resolved. Still, acid is easily available in open markets. Many women are being raped every day. Many married women are enduring domestic abuse behind closed doors. Gender-based atrocities are consistently hindering the progress of women in society. Though strict laws are definitely a very good step to address this societal issue, they are not enough. Of course, gaps exist between policy formulation and implementation. Therefore, it is required to work on minimisation of these gaps, improvise legal infrastructure, exterminate the typical stereotypes of societal beliefs and attitudes, and undertake policies for the advancement of the immediate situational environment. The measures suggested in this study after a deep consideration of individual crime events would assist law enforcement officials in effectively addressing this societal issue. Proper vigilance in the porous border areas, proper resource utilisation, generating employment opportunities, increasing more work participation, poverty alleviation, ensuring food securities, ameliorating the neighbourhood's social ties, increasing awareness, and, above all, educating the local inhabitants, would help reduce the large-scale social disorganisation in society, annihilate socio-economic imbalances, and address gender-based atrocities to a great extent. This study strongly advises lessening gender discrimination in society. Attempts should be made to change the traditional patriarchal beliefs and attitudes that suppress women's progress in all spheres of life and force them to accept violence. A transformation in societal attitudes towards women would enhance their self-esteem and dignity and help them to get acquainted with their legal rights. It would not be possible unless the government and the NGOs extended their hands and support. Rigorous awareness about changing societal attitudes, ensuring more women's work participation, strengthening laws, and, above all, ensuring women's education are highly needed.

Thus, this study might contribute to a better understanding of crime patterns in order to support better policing for practitioners by limiting opportunities (*O*) (e.g., more patrolling, CCTV surveillance, more street lights, improving neighbourhood connotation, mass awareness), increasing risk (*R*) (e.g., risk of being caught), increasing effort (*E*), and reducing payoff (*P*) so that women in society could live with dignity and honour and a crime-free society could be developed.

Appendix 1

Summarisation of Some
Published Newspaper Reports
Concerning Women Trafficking
in South-24 Parganas District

Source	Rescue from	Destination	Path	Age of victim	Offender Identity	Year	Reason	No of victims	Under police station of	District	Hyperlink
Bhangor	Delhi	Delhi	Howrah	19	Rishi Raj (trafficker)	2017	On the pretext of marriage and also lured by getting job adjoining to Noida	1	Bhangor	South-24 Parganas	httPS://timesofindia.indiatimes.com/city/kolkata/19-year-old-trafficked-girl-rescued-from-delhi/articleshow/57190533.cms
Bansberia		Chapra, Bihar	Howrah	15	Neighbours	2015	Dancing	1	Mograhat PS	South-24 Parganas	httPS://www.anandabazar.com/district/howrah-hoogly/bansberia-girl-rescued-from-chhapra-bihar-1.160273
Baruipur	Gajiabad, Delhi	Gajiabad, Delhi	Howrah via Sealdah	22	Lover	2015	Promise of marriage	1	Baruipur	South-24 Parganas	httPS://www.anandabazar.com/state/youth-sold-lady-love-to-women-traffickers-by-1-5-lakh-rupees-later-rescued-by-cid-1.219999

(Continued)

(Continued)

Source	Rescue from	Destination	Path	Age of victim	Offender Identity	Year	Reason	No of victims	Under police station of	District	Hyperlink
Bangladesh	Bandar area brick ling field, Habra	Mumbai	Bashirhat Simanto	15	Rubel Dewan (trafficker)	2016	Promise of marriage	1	Habra, Bandar	South-24 Parganas	httPS://www.anandabazar.com/district/24-parganas/women-trafficking-situation-getting-worse-day-by-day-at-bongaon-1.480402
Canning (taldir)		UP (Khusinagar)	Howrah via Sealdah		Payel Haldar and Biswajit Haldar (trafficker)	2017		1	Canning PS	South-24 Parganas	httPS://www.anandabazar.com/district/24-paraganas/4-girls-rescued-from-trafficking-1.523305
Joynagar		Haryana (Rohtak area)			Husband and a relatives named Ruhul Kuddus Gaji			1	Canning P.s,and Joynagar PS	South-24 Parganas	httPS://www.anandabazar.com/district/24-paraganas/4-girls-rescued-from-trafficking-1.523305
Jibontala		Delhi (Rajouri Garden),up,	Howrah via Sealdah		Neighbours		Promise for job	1	Jibantala PS	South-24 Parganas	httPS://www.anandabazar.com/district/24-paraganas/4-girls-rescued-from-trafficking-1.523305

Mathurapur	Agra	Agra	Howrah via Sealdah	15	Lover	2017	Marriage proposal	1	Mathurapur	South-24 Parganas	httPS://www.anandabazar.com/district/24-paraganas/charges-filed-against-human-trafficking-1.622983
Canning	Delhi	Delhi			Mother	2016	Mother sold girl	1	Canning PS	South-24 Parganas	httPS://www.anandabazar.com/district/24-paraganas/woman-arrested-for-girl-trafficking-at-canning-1.494690
Sagar	Gobindapuri, Delhi	Gobindapuri, Delhi			Lover	2017	Marriage proposal	1	Sagar PS and Basanti PS	South-24 Parganas	httPS://www.anandabazar.com/district/24-paraganas/girl-saved-before-trafficking-1.542517
Canning	Pune	Pune	Howrah via Sealdah	Unknown Neighbours		2017	Prostitution	1	Canning PS	South-24 Parganas	httPS://www.anandabazar.com/state/another-ayesha-from-bengal-with-serious-injury-identified-from-delhi-1.606004

(*Continued*)

(Continued)

Source	Rescue from	Destination	Path	Age of victim	Offender Identity	Year	Reason	No of victims	Under police station of	District	Hyperlink
Maheshtala PS	Delhi	Delhi	Sealdah	15	Neighbours	2017	Marriage trafficking	1	Maheshtala PS	South-24 Parganas	httPS://www. anandabazar. com/state/ threat-of-trafficking-again-the-lady-is-fighting-who-saved-her-life-from-being-sold-1.582931
Diamond harbour	Delhi G.B. PantRoad brothel	Delhi G.B. Pant Road brothel	Howrah	15	Unknown	2015	Prostitution	1	Diamond harbour	South-24 Parganas	httPS://www. anandabazar. com/national/ police-took-class-at-school-to-stop-the-girl-s-kidnapping-1.537602
Joynagar	Bihar, Siwan area	Siwan, Bihar	Howrah	16	Neighbour	2017	Prostitution	1	Joynagar PS	South-24 Parganas	httPS://www. anandabazar. com/state/sex-workers-choose-to-finish-their-life-as-their-rehabilitation-does-not-happen-properly-1.712374

Joynagar	Pune	Howrah	16	Monirul Molla (neighbour)	2017	Dancing	1	Joynagar PS	South-24 Parganas	httPS://www.anandabazar.com/state/teenage-student-rescued-after-getting-kidnapped-but-still-child-traffickers-are-threatening-her-1.676567
Mahestala	Pune	Howrah	15	Neighbours	2017	Prostitution	1	Maheshtala PS	South-24 Parganas	httPS://www.anandabazar.com/state/threat-of-trafficking-again-the-lady-is-fighting-who-saved-her-life-from-being-sold-1.582931
Nafarganj, Basanti	Gobindapuri, Delhi	Gobindapuri, Delhi	Howrah via Sealdah	13	Unknown	2016	Prostitution	1	Canning PS	South-24 Parganas	httPS://www.anandabazar.com/district/24-paraganas/women-trafficking-from-sunderban-is-increasing-1.481071

(*Continued*)

(Continued)

Source	Rescue from	Destination	Path	Age of victim	Offender Identity	Year	Reason	No of victims	Under police station of	District	Hyperlink
Joynagar	Mumbai	Mumbai	Howrah	25		2016	Prostitution	1	Joynagar	South-24 Parganas	httPS://www. anandabazar. com/district/24-paraganas/women-traffick-ing-from-sunder-ban-is-increas-ing-1.481071
Sundarbans	Mumbai	Mumbai	Howrah	21	Lover	2016	Prostitution	1	Sundarbans PS	South-24 Parganas	httPS://www. anandabazar. com/district/24-paraganas/women-traffick-ing-from-sunder-ban-is-increas-ing-1.481071

Source: Anandabazar Patrika and The Times of India.

Appendix 2

Factor Loading of Determinants
of Trafficking in South-24
Parganas

Variables Measures	Cronbach Alpha, α	Component						
		Factor 1	Factor 2	Factor 3	Factor 4	Factor 5	Factor 6	Factor 7
		Status of Education	Poverty and Unemployment	Environmentally Vulnerable Area	Lack of Basic Amenities	Sociopolitical Background and Influence of Social Media	Gender Discrimination	National and International Borders and Migration
The parents of school dropout girls engaged them in household works		0.865						
Literacy rate among people in this region is low		0.862						
Intensity of school dropout among the female students is high here		0.86						
Illiteracy or having limited educational qualification of the girls and women limits the power of judging what is good or what is harmful to them		0.854						

Illiteracy leads to unawareness about trafficking activities		0.835
The existence of situations of abuse in family influences girls and women to take risky decision to migrate		0.829
Many of the poor and illiterate families are unaware about human trafficking		0.829
In those families where parents do not have good relation with their children, there is possibility of children being misguided by the children traffickers		0.825
The poor and illiterate families having many girl children are the sole target of the traffickers to lure them to send their daughters outside for better earning	0.987	0.824

(Continued)

(Continued)

Variables Measures	Cronbach Alpha, α	Component						
		Factor 1	Factor 2	Factor 3	Factor 4	Factor 5	Factor 6	Factor 7
		Status of Education	Poverty and Unemployment	Environmentally Vulnerable Area	Lack of Basic Amenities	Sociopolitical Background and Influence of Social Media	Gender Discrimination	National and International Borders and Migration
It is easy for the agents to tempt the alcohol/drug addicted parents to send their daughters in cities		0.82						
Education helps to improve skills		0.806						
Limited educational qualification limits the opportunities of government and non-governmental jobs to the women within their locality		0.791						
Illiterate parents' get lured easily by better job opportunities or marriage proposals of their daughters		0.549						

	Invalid	Invalid	Invalid	Invalid	Invalid	Invalid	Invalid	Invalid
The ferry system is inadequate in areas where the boat is the means of transport	Invalid							
Poverty push women to undertake decision of risky migration for doing job in cities	.910							
Number of non-working population is high in this region	.901							
Because of acute poverty parents agreed to send their daughters with the agents for better earning	.896							
The job card is not available to every working population	.889							
Desire for modern lifestyle among the poor girls is high in this region	0.887							
In the outer region, wages are high compared to your locality	0.886							

(Continued)

(Continued)

Variables Measures	Cronbach Alpha, α	Component						
		Factor 1	Factor 2	Factor 3	Factor 4	Factor 5	Factor 6	Factor 7
		Status of Education	*Poverty and Unemployment*	*Environmentally Vulnerable Area*	*Lack of Basic Amenities*	*Sociopolitical Background and Influence of Social Media*	*Gender Discrimination*	*National and International Borders and Migration*
In your locality maximum people belong to Below Poverty Level (BPL) category			0.883					
Job opportunities are very less here			0.88					
Due to extreme poverty situations the poor parents' arranged marriage for their daughters at early age without verifying the identity of the groom properly			0.877					
Due to extreme poverty, it become difficult for the parents to educate their daughters			0.876					

Less job opportunities forced people to migrate city region for better earning	0.868
Due to frequent cyclones and tidal floods agricultural fields loss its productivity	0.881
During the time of severe flood entire deltaic region remain detached from the mainland and its effects on their economy and livelihood as well	0.872
In this deltaic region, natural calamities like floods, cyclones, tidal surges are very much frequent.	0.866
Severe natural calamities limit the livelihood opportunities to the habitats in the deltaic region	0.863

(Continued)

(Continued)

Variables Measures	Cronbach Alpha, α	Component						
		Factor 1	Factor 2	Factor 3	Factor 4	Factor 5	Factor 6	Factor 7
		Status of Education	Poverty and Unemployment	Environmentally Vulnerable Area	Lack of Basic Amenities	Sociopolitical Background and Influence of Social Media	Gender Discrimination	National and International Borders and Migration
Traffickers take advantage of the aftermath situations of climatic hazards and lure the poor parents to send their daughters in cities for better earning				0.862				
Due to frequent cyclonic hazards, most of the poor farmers sold their agricultural land to the Dalal's or private companies at a very minimum cost				0.852				
Due to frequent cyclones and tidal floods soil and water get contaminated				0.847				

Such a hazardous environment forced people to migrate economically well-off region for better livelihood opportunities	0.824	
In this region, health infrastructure is not well		0.788
Numbers of the primary and secondary schools are not adequate in number here.		0.776
The lack of other basic facilities in this region is noticed	0.772	
Drinking water getting contaminated due to the tidal surges in many areas	0.722	
The infrastructure of higher education is not adequate here	0.72	

(Continued)

(Continued)

Variables Measures	Cronbach Alpha, α	Component						
		Factor 1	Factor 2	Factor 3	Factor 4	Factor 5	Factor 6	Factor 7
		Status of Education	Poverty and Unemployment	Environmentally Vulnerable Area	Lack of Basic Amenities	Sociopolitical Background and Influence of Social Media	Gender Discrimination	National and International Borders and Migration
Improper sanitation facilities are noticed in many villages in this region				.711				
Not all the region (where road connection is possible) are well connected by pucca road here					0.674			
Use of solar electricity seems to be costly to many of the poor families					0.667			
Villagers have to go more than 300 metres from home to collect drinking water					0.647			

Public Distribution Systems (PDS) is not properly distributed here	0.616	
Drinking water facilities are not adequate here	0.556	
Electricity is not reached in many villages of the Sundarbans region	0.516	
The cultural belief of early age of marriage of girls in society is one of the most useful modes of trafficking		0.812
Due to the ineffectiveness of law enforcement authorities in this region, the traffickers do illicit activities fearlessly		0.81
It is quite easy to build a fake friendship with young girls through social media		0.802

(Continued)

(Continued)

Variables Measures	Cronbach Alpha, α	Component						
		Factor 1	Factor 2	Factor 3	Factor 4	Factor 5	Factor 6	Factor 7
		Status of Education	*Poverty and Unemployment*	*Environmentally Vulnerable Area*	*Lack of Basic Amenities*	*Sociopolitical Background and Influence of Social Media*	*Gender Discrimination*	*National and International Borders and Migration*
Girls belong to deprive community (SC, ST, other minority groups) are more vulnerable to trafficking						0.789		
It can be difficult to properly know about a person through social media						0.785		
In recent days young girls are addicted to social and electronic media						0.785		
Frequent political turmoil situations result in the marginalization of many families and enhance the possibilities of trafficking						.774		

Social ties get falling down due to the adverse effects of social and electronic media	.764	
Girls do not want to share about their new friendship (fake) with their nearest one	.677	
The patriarchal society tries to remain free from all responsibilities by giving their daughters marriage at an early age.		0.67
Women have no scope to express their choices in the family		0.655
In the family males take all the important decisions		0.651
Women seems to be subordinate to men in society		0.648
It is quite easy to migrate illegally along the natural border		0.722

(Continued)

(Continued)

142   *Appendix 2: Factor Loading of Determinants of Trafficking*

Variables Measures	Cronbach Alpha, α	Component						
		Factor 1 Status of Education	Factor 2 Poverty and Unemployment	Factor 3 Environmentally Vulnerable Area	Factor 4 Lack of Basic Amenities	Factor 5 Sociopolitical Background and Influence of Social Media	Factor 6 Gender Discrimination	Factor 7 National and International Borders and Migration
Along the international border illegal migration continue to occur								0.713
For its locational advantages (in terms of sharing an international border), it helps the traffickers to use this deltaic region as one of the major sources as well as transit area of trafficking								0.693
Eigen value		11.92	11.42	8.93	8.67	7.72	2.51	2.21
% Of Variance		19.54	18.71	14.63	14.21	12.65	4.11	3.62
Cumulative %		19.54	38.25	52.89	67.10	79.75	83.87	**87.49**

Notes: Extraction method: Principal Component Analysis.
Rotation Method: Varimax with Kaiser normalisation.
aRotation converged in seven iterations.

Appendix 3

District-wise Recorded Incidences of Acid Attacks in West Bengal (2010–2017)

Districts	Year								
	2010	*2011*	*2012*	*2013*	*2014*	*2015*	*2016*	*2017*	*Total*
Alipur Duwar					1			1	2
Bankura					1			1	2
Birbhum		1			2			1	4
Burdwan					2	1	3	3	9
Cooch Behar						2			2
Howrah		1						1	2
Hooghly			1	1	4	1	1		8
Jalpaiguri					1			1	2
Kolkata	1			1	1			1	4
Malda			1		1	1			3
Murshidabad		1	2		2		1		6
N-24 Pargana	1			1	1		2	2	7
Nadia			1		1		3		5
Paschim Medinipur						2	2	5	9
Purba Medinipur				1	3			1	5
South Dinajpur					1		1		2
S-24 Pargana	1		1		1	1	1	3	8
Uttar Dinajpur					1				1
Total									**81**

Low rate	Medium rate	High rate	Very high rate

Source: Newspaper reports (*The Times of India* and *Anandabazar Patrika*) and ASFI records. (Modified after Biswas and Chatterjee, 2018.)

Appendix 4

Reliability Statistics of All Variables

Cronbach's Alpha	Cronbach's Alpha Based on Standardised Items	No. of Items
.879	.885	19

Source: Computed by author.

Appendix 5

KMO and Bartlett's Test

Kaiser–Meyer–Olkin Measure of Sampling Adequacy		**0.801**
Bartlett's Test of Sphericity	Approx. Chi-square	5,271.468
	df	171
	Sig.	.000

Source: Computed by author.

Appendix 6

Factor Loading of Determinants
of Acid Attacks

Variables Measures	Cronbach Alpha, α	Component			
		Factor 1	Factor 2	Factor 3	Factor 4
		Rejection of Marriage and Love Proposal	*Easy and Cheap Availability of Acid in Open Markets*	*Marital Disputes, Domestic Violence, and Dowry*	*Low Educational Status*
• Men always try to control over women		.927			
• Rejection by women hits men's ego, so they attack women with acid to take revenge		.922			
• Women have the right to avoid unwanted peoples	0.972	.904			
• Most of the incidences of acid attacks happen due to the refusal of the suitors' proposals		.890			
• Women must have their own choices to decide whom to talk		.880			
• Women have the right to reject suitors' love or marriage proposals		.836			
• Safety must be maintained to store acid at home or in any business store			.993		
• Sellers rarely maintain registrar copy			.992		
• The easy availability of acid increases the likelihood of heinous criminal activity of acid attack	0.989		.992		
• Acid is widely used in household work like toilet cleaner and other works			.970		
• Acid is readily available at local stores			.960		

(Continued)

(Continued)

Variables Measures	Cronbach Alpha, a	Component			
		Factor 1	Factor 2	Factor 3	Factor 4
		Rejection of Marriage and Love Proposal	*Easy and Cheap Availability of Acid in Open Markets*	*Marital Disputes, Domestic Violence, and Dowry*	*Low Educational Status*
• Domestic violence against women is very common in every household in West Bengal				.891	
• In many families, marital disputes can be noticed				.885	
• Women should always obey their husband and in-laws	0.966			.882	
• Dowry is largely accountable for domestic violence victimisation among women				.858	
• Nowadays throwing acid on the face is one of the weapons to punish a wife or daughter-in-law				.853	
• Lower educational levels affect crime					.953
• Education helps to improve self-control	0.917				.919
• Education improves people's morality					.900
Eigenvalue		5.398	4.831	4.348	2.591
% of variance		**28.411**	25.426	22.886	13.637
Cumulative %		28.411	53.837	76.724	90.361

Notes: Extraction method: principal component analysis.
Rotation method: varimax with Kaiser normalisation.
[a]Rotation converged in five iterations.
Source: Author's computation.

Appendix 7

Factor Loading of Determinants
of Rape and Sexual Abuse

Variables Measures	Reliability Statistics		Component (Rotated Component Matrix^a)				
	Cronbach's Alpha (No. of Items = 38)		Factor 1	Factor 2	Factor 3	Factor 4	Factor 5
	All Variables	Group Variables	Societal Foster Beliefs and Attitudes	Individual Perpetrator's Attitude and Socio-economic Adversity	Relationship Factors	Legal and Deterrence Factors	Adverse Physical Environment
Societal foster beliefs of perceived male superiority and sexual entitlement	.986	.995	0.917				
Family honour considered more important than safety of girls endorse more victimization of rape			0.907				
Societal norms that foster the beliefs of women's inferiority and sexual submissiveness			0.907	0.995			
Poor neighbourhood connections			0.904				
General tolerance attitude towards sexual annoyance within the community /society			0.902	1			
Societal stereotype belief and myths about rape			0.9				

Weak community sanctions against the culprits of sexual assaults	0.891
Less educated women in society are less likely to report rape which encourages the culprits to do offence fearlessly	0.878
Broader social support of sexual violence	.878
Existence of high level of criminal annoyance in the community/ society	.875
Deep rooted patriarchal beliefs present in Indian society that grant male dominance over female behaviour	0.907
Strong notion of masculinity linked to dominance, honour, or aggression	0.868
Less education among people in a society reduce moral restrain of individuals which turn affects the decision to engage in criminal activities	0.858

(Continued)

(Continued)

Variables Measures	Reliability Statistics		Component (Rotated Component Matrix[a])				
	Cronbach's Alpha (No. of Items = 38)		Factor 1	Factor 2	Factor 3	Factor 4	Factor 5
	All Variables	Group Variables	Societal Foster Beliefs and Attitudes	Individual Perpetrator's Attitude and Socio-economic Adversity	Relationship Factors	Legal and Deterrence Factors	Adverse Physical Environment
Community associating with sexuality aggressive peoples or neighbours			0.856				
Impulsive and antisocial tendencies				.888			
Perpetrators follow the routine activities of their targets				.885			
Lack of education and moral restrain among perpetrators				.884			
Rapes are indeed committed disproportionately by men with substandard socio-economic status				.879			
Witnessing family violence as a child				.877			
Childhood history of physical, sexual, or psychological victimization				0.876			

Extreme unemployment and poverty situations endorsed criminal activities in society	0.872	
Men engage in sexual atrocities irrespective of all socio-economic status	0.859	
General aggressiveness and attitudes supportive of sexual violence	0.853	
Adherence to traditional gender role norms	0.733	
Alcohol, drug, or other substance abuse	0.725	
Involvement in a violent or abusive intimate relationship		.823
Weak parent–child relation in family		.815
Nourish in a family environment characterized by frequent conflicts, tension and physical violence		.763
Strong patriarchal environment in family		.742

(Continued)

(Continued)

Variables Measures	Reliability Statistics		Component (Rotated Component Matrix^a)				
	Cronbach's Alpha (No. of Items = 38)		Factor 1	Factor 2	Factor 3	Factor 4	Factor 5
	All Variables	Group Variables	Societal Foster Beliefs and Attitudes	Individual Perpetrator's Attitude and Socio-economic Adversity	Relationship Factors	Legal and Deterrence Factors	Adverse Physical Environment
Associates with sexually aggressive, hyper-masculine, and delinquent peers					.714		
Emotionally unsupportive family environment					.684		
Weak laws and policies related to sexual annoyance						0.758	
Lengthen judicial procedures for punishing the rapists						0.751	
Lack of institutional support (from community, police and judicial system) to the victims						0.742	
Insufficient legal interventions						0.73	
Lack of street lights endorsed the victimization of rape							0.815

Abandoned areas (i.e., closed industrial areas, mining areas, brick kiln fields, closed tea estates and so on) are not safe for women					0.814
International border areas in West Bengal are not safe for women (illegal migration and occurrence of other illicit activities are much there)					0.773
Eigen value	13.28	10.42	5.27	3.2	2.79
% Of Variance	34.96	27.42	13.88	8.42	7.34
Cumulative %	34.96	62.37	76.25	84.67	92.02

Notes: Extraction method: principal component analysis.
Rotation method: varimax with Kaiser normalisation.
[a]Rotation converged in six iterations.
Source: Computed by author.

Appendix 8

Differentials of Domestic Violence Experienced by Ever Married Women since the Past 12 Months by Selected Background Characteristics ($N = 864$)

Socio-demographic Indicators	Experiences of Domestic Violence in the Past 12 Months, n (%)		p-Value
	Yes (n = 669)	No (n = 195)	
Age of women (years)			
15–18	193 (88.8)	24 (11.1)	***
19–29	176 (87.1)	26 (12.9)	***
30–39	156 (70.6)	65 (29.4)	***
40–49	144 (64.3)	80 (35.7)	***
Education			
No or primary level	311 (98.1)	6 (1.9)	***
Secondary and HS levels	304 (76.0)	96(24.0)	***
Graduation and above	54 (36.7)	93 (63.3)	***
Age at marriage (years)			
Up to 18	493 (95.4)	24 (4.6)	***
19–24	170 (63.9)	96 (36.1)	***
25 and above	6 (7.4)	75 (92.6)	***
Community of origin			
Urban	235 (64.4)	130 (35.6)	***
Rural	434 (87.0)	65 (13.0)	***
Occupation			
Housewife	517 (88.5)	67 (11.5)	***
Salaried job	23 (24.0)	73 (76.0)	***
Self-employed	129 (70.1)	55 (29.9)	***
Economic conditions			
Low economic class	300 (90.4)	32 (9.6)	***
Medium economic class	250 (78.4)	69 (21.6)	***
High economic class	119 (55.9)	94 (44.1)	***
Child sex			
No child	237 (95.6)	11 (4.4)	***
Son (s) only	12 (11.1)	96 (88.9)	***
Daughter (s) only	338 (95.8)	15 (4,2)	***

(Continued)

(Continued)

Socio-demographic Indicators	Experiences of Domestic Violence in the Past 12 Months, n (%)		p-Value
	Yes (n = 669)	No (n = 195)	
Both	82 (52.9)	73 (47.1)	***
Household head sex			
Male	557 (86.6)	86 (13.4)	***
Female	112 (50.7)	109 (49.3)	***
Acceptance			
Agree	548 (88.8)	69 (11.2)	***
Sometimes	18 (69.2)	8 (30.8)	***
Disagree	103 (46.6)	118 (53.4)	***
Legal Awareness			
Yes	66 (40.2)	98 (59.8)	***
Somewhat	111 (56.3)	86 (43.7)	***
No	492 (97.8)	11 (2.2)	***
Confront			
Never	435 (96.5)	16 (3.5)	***
Sometimes	155 (73.5)	56 (26.5)	***
Always	79 (39.1)	123 (60.9)	***

Note ***$p < 0.001$
Source: Author computation.

Appendix 9

Factors Associated with Women (Ever Married) Experience of Domestic Violence by Selected Background Characteristics (*N* = 864)

Socio-demographic Indicators	Experiences of Domestic Violence (Predicted Probability Is of Membership for No)	P-value
	Adjusted Odds Ratio (aOR) (95% CI)	
Age of women (years)		
40–49	Reference	
30–39	1.188 [658, 2.146]	ns
19–29	3.351 [2.005, 5.599]	***
15–18	4.468 [2.697, 7.400]	***
Education		
Graduation and above	Reference	
Secondary and HS level	16.368 [7.068, 37.907]	***
No or primary level	89.269 [37.225, 214.072]	***
Age at marriage (years)		
25 and above	Reference	***
19–24	11.600 [7.177, 18.748]	***
Up to 18	256.771 [101.61, 648.83]	***
Community of origin		
Rural	Reference	
Urban	.271 [.193, .379]	***
Occupation		
Salaried job	Reference	
Housewife	1.629 [1.118., 2.371]	**
Self-employed	2.117 [1.389, 3.228]	***
Economic conditions		
High-economic class	Reference	***
Medium economic class	2.587 [1.647, 4.064]	***
Low economic class	7.405 [4.704, 11.659]	***
Child sex		

(*Continued*)

(Continued)

Socio-demographic Indicators	Experiences of Domestic Violence (Predicted Probability Is of Membership for No)	P-value
	Adjusted Odds Ratio (aOR) (95% CI)	
Son(s) only	Reference	
Daughter(s) only	40.652 [20.387, 81.016]	***
Both	.798 [.340, 1.873]	ns
No child	19.181 [9.699, 37.930]	***
Household head sex		
Female	Reference	
Male	2.197 [1.589, 3.036]	***
Acceptance		
Disagree	Reference	
Sometimes	12.101 [7.691, 19.040]	***
Agree	2.725 [1.827, 4.062]	***
Legal Awareness		
No	Reference	
Somewhat	.399 [.265, .602]	***
Yes	.016 [.008, .032]	***
Confront		
Always	Reference	
Sometimes	8.603 [4.787, 15.460]	***
Never	22.022 [12.617, 38.439]	***
Naglekerke *R*(for gross effects)	.819	

Note: ***p<0.001; ** = *p* < 0.05; CI = confidence interval; ns = not significant.
Source: Author computation

Appendix 10

KMO and Bartlett's Test Result

Kaiser–Meyer–Olkin Measure of Sampling Adequacy		.560
Bartlett's Test of Sphericity	Approx. chi-square	97.974
	Df	45
	Sig.	**.000**

Source: Author computation.

Appendix 11

Factor Loading of Determinants of Crime against Women

Variables	Component (Rotated Component Matrix^a)			
	Factor 1	Factor 2	Factor 3	Factor 4
	Socio-economic Adversity and Disorganisation	Population Inflow, Gender Imparity and Social Disorganisation	Socio-Demographic Indicators and Emerging Issues	Lack of Basic Amenities and Consequence Social Disorder
Literacy rate	0.972			
HDI	0.878			
HPI	−0.875			
School enrolment ratio		0.867		
Gender gap		0.610		
Per capita income		−0.592		
No. of immigrants		0.555		
Sex ratio			0.925	
Population density			−0.859	
Availability of basic amenities				−0.911
Eigenvalue	3.148	1.843	1.84	1.256
% of Variance	31.478	18.428	18.399	12.558
Cumulative %	31.478	49.906	68.306	**80.863**

Notes: Extraction method: principal component analysis.
Rotation method: varimax with Kaiser normalisation. ^aRotation converged in six iterations.
Source: Author computation.

Index

Note: Page numbers in *italics* indicate a figure and page numbers in **bold** indicate a table on the corresponding page.

For Product Safety Concerns and Information please contact our EU
representative GPSR@taylorandfrancis.com
Taylor & Francis Verlag GmbH, Kaufingerstraße 24, 80331 München, Germany